The New
John G. Lake Sermons

by Gordon Lindsay

Published By
CHRIST FOR THE NATIONS INC.
Dallas, Texas
Reprint 2006
All Rights Reserved

CONTENTS

Printed by Printcorp. LP # 02330/0056863 of 30.04.2004.
Minsk, Belarus. Ord. 616 (06112A). Qty 3000.

CHAPTER I

The Second Crowning

"And I saw in the right hand of him that sat on the throne a book written within and on the backside, sealed with seven seals. And I saw a strong angel proclaiming with a loud voice, Who is worthy to open the book, and to loose the seals thereof? And no man in heaven, nor in earth, neither under the earth, was able to open the book, neither to look thereon. And I wept much, because no man was found worthy to open and to read the book, neither to look thereon. And one of the elders saith unto me, Weep not: behold, the Lion of the tribe of Juda, the Root of David, hath prevailed to open the book, and to loose the seven seals thereof. And I beheld, and, lo, in the midst of the throne and of the four beasts, and in the midst of the elders, stood a Lamb as it had been slain, having seven horns and seven eyes, which are the seven Spirits of God sent forth into all the earth. And he came and took the book out of the right hand of him that sat upon the throne" (Rev. 5:1-7).

Somehow the minds of men the world over have ever been concentrated around the cross of Christ. One of the strangest things to me in all Christian life has been the manner in which the souls of men cling to the cross of Calvary. And I have sometimes felt that it is one of the great reasons why there has been so little progress made in the higher Christian life.

While we revere the cross of Calvary, and while the soul of man will ever love to think of Him Who gave His life for us, yet I believe the triumph of the Christ began at the cross and ends only when the race like Himself has received from God the Father, through Him, the grace, power and glory of God that makes them sons of God like Himself.

It is a long way between the cross of Calvary and the throne of God, but that is the way Jesus traveled and that is the course for every other soul of man. I am glad that God is never hurried. He

3

has plenty of time. A few years make much difference in this life, but God has plenty of time for the elevation of the soul, for the perfect tuition of every heart, until that heart comes into such complete and perfect unison that the nature of man is absolutely changed into the nature of Christ.

The triumph of Jesus, as we see it outlined in the Scriptures, has always been one of the splendid inspirations of my own soul. It seems to me if we had not been permitted to have that foreview of that final triumph of the Son of God, there might have been the conception in the minds of many that after all the life and death of our Lord Jesus Christ was not the perfect triumph that it ought to have been. It seems, therefore, that no one can have the highest appreciation of the real Christian life and the consciousness that real Christianity brings, unless he can see the triumph of the Christ.

If we stop to think that one-half of the great Christian world is still carrying a little cross representing a dead Christ, we will realize how the mind of man is yet chained to the cross of Calvary to a dead Christ, to a tomb—not empty—but the tomb that contains the One they love.

Beloved, that is not Christianity. Christianity is the ringing triumph of the mind of God. It is the blessed victory that the individual feels in his own heart of the consciousness of the presence and power of God within the soul which makes man the master now, and gives him the consciousness of mastery over sin and over the powers of sickness and death.

I have always wondered how a Christian could be any less than an optimist. It is a sad thing when you hear Christians groan in their soul. When I meet the groaner, I say in my heart: "God move the man on into the place where he comprehends what Christianity is."

In my early boyhood we worshipped in a little old church where the saints were having a hard time. I remember when the dear class leader one day said, "It seems such a short time since I was a boy, and now I am on the western slope of the hill, halfway down." And he stopped and sniffed the air in a peculiar kind of way. To him there was nothing but gloom ahead.

The Christian with a groan in him never moved the world except to more groans. In a divine healing meeting some months ago, as I was teaching, I tried to develop the thought that as a man thinketh in his heart, so is he. And I was endeavoring to show the people that the spirit of victory in Christ Jesus in one's heart not only

4

affected the attitude of one's mind, but likewise his soul too. In fact, through the nervous system man's mental attitudes are transmitted clear through the body.

The attitude of our soul has much to do not only with our mental status and our spiritual life, but likewise with our physical health. Indeed it seems to me that as the spirit of man is tuned with God, all the outgrowth of his life will be in harmony with his spirit. The attitude of the mind will be in accordance, and the condition of the body will be a revelation of the attitude of his mind. That is the reason why I have always endeavored in my preaching to bring before the mind of man the consciousness of triumph, the consciousness of victory, the power of mastery. It seems to me there is a great deal of superficial endeavor in the world to pump one's self up, similar to a man taking himself by the bootstraps and trying to lift himself over the fence.

We speak of mastery, not because we are endeavoring to lift our consciousness into the place where we can possibly conceive of mastery, but because the spirit of mastery is born within the heart. The real Christian is a royal fighter. He is one who loves to enter into the contest with his whole soul and take the situation captive for the Lord Jesus Christ.

When by the grace and power of the Son of God, you and I yield ourselves to God until our nature becomes the possessor of the Spirit that is in Christ, then we begin to realize the spirit of mastery that Jesus possessed when He said, "I am he that liveth and was dead; and, behold, I am alive forevermore, Amen; and have the keys of hell and of death."

That is the reason I do not spend much time talking about the devil. The Lord took care of him, bless God! He has the keys of death and hell, and He has mastered that condition once and for all. If you and I had as much faith to believe it as we have to believe that the Lord Jesus is our Saviour, we would have little trouble with the devil while we walk through this world.

It is a hard thing for the Christian mind to conceive that the power of evil is really a vanquished power. When I think of examples of Christian triumph, my mind very frequently reverts to a certain minister. He was a great soul. The dominion of Christ seemed to dwell within him intensely. I was with him on one occasion when he was called to a dying man down in the slums. It was always interesting to me to watch the sparkle of his eye. I asked, "Brother, do you know anything about this man's condition?"

5

"Well," he replied, "the messenger told me the man was in a state of great suffering and likely to die. But, he is not going to die." I answered, "Amen."

You see, there was a ring of conscious mastery in his soul that made it possible for such a burst of confidence to come from his spirit. I said to myself, "There is not going to be much difficulty tonight. The fellow has the victory in his soul in advance." When we finally knelt by the man's side and the minister put his hands on him and called on the mighty God to deliver the man, I felt the flash of his spirit; and I knew before I arose from my knees that the man was healed. And he was!

There are times when it seems to me it is not fitting even to pray. There is a life of praise. Once while in conversation with Dr. Myland, the pastor of the Christian and Missionary Alliance Church at Columbus, Ohio, I happened to mention the fact that I had not prayed concerning a personal matter. Turning to me he remarked, "I have not prayed for myself for four years." That sounded very strange to me at that time. I did not understand. He added, "No, I passed beyond the place of praying, brother, into the place where I was ready to accept what the Lord Jesus Christ has wrought and to receive the power of His Spirit in my life so that the thing that He has wrought for me should become evident through me." And the man had walked for four years in that continuous victory!

An hour of consternation came to the prophet John as God unfolded to him that which was to occur in the future. A book appears, a marvelous book, sealed with seven seals. An angel with a trumpet voice proceeds to utter a proclamation, "Who is worthy to open the book, and to loose the seals thereof?" And mankind stood dumfounded. No man in heaven nor on earth, was able to loose the seals nor to open the book. And it seemed to the prophet as if a great disappointment were at hand. He says, "I wept much." But presently the angel guide spoke to him, "Weep not: behold, the Lion of the tribe of Juda, the Root of David, hath prevailed to open the book." John says, "I beheld . . . a Lamb." Blessed be God. The real overcomer does not always evidence his overcoming power with much noise. In this case his overcoming was in the consciousness that was in his heart. He was as a Lamb, gentle, sweet, loving, tender, and true.

But the consciousness of power was there. When others stood dumfounded, when others stood baffled, the Christ appears. He takes the book, opens the seals and discusses its contents. Beloved,

6

the triumph of the Christ of God is not necessarily the triumph of loud shouting. It is the triumph of what you know in your soul.

How often have you and I walked into the presence of a man whose calmness gave instant strength. How often in life when the minds of men were driven to confusion, have we seen a single soul maintain his poise in God, and become a balancing power in society? History records that at the death of Lincoln, when the news of his assassination became known in New York, the city was almost on the point of breaking into a riot. Three men lay dead in the streets when James A. Garfield appeared on the veranda of one of the hotels. Raising his hands, he spoke these simple words, which brought calm on the whole mob, and the whole city, and was transferred over the nation, "God is our king, and the government at Washington still lives." The storm was over as when Jesus spoke the marvelous words: "Peace be still." There flowed over the nation the calm of poise in God.

It is said that the day following the great Chicago fire, two hundred men committed suicide in that city. The old *Chicago Tribune* came out with a big red-letter headline: "Any Coward Can Commit Suicide, But It Takes a Man to Live Under These Conditions." And the whole thing stopped. There were no more suicides. The wave of cowardice was broken up. The consciousness of one great soul who had the poise of God within his heart, was able by the grace of God to transmit it to other lives.

Most of our difficulties are the difficulties that we anticipate or fear are coming tomorrow. The world is in consternation concerning tomorrow, or the next day, or the next day. Jesus said, "Sufficient unto the day is the evil thereof." Do not worry about tomorrow. Rest down in God. The mighty arms of the living God will be underneath tomorrow, just as they are today.

If I could bring to you today one blessing greater than another, it would be the consciousness of trust in God. "Fear not, neither be thou afraid, for I the Lord thy God am with thee whithersoever thou goest."

Over there is a little woman who came into the healing rooms recently weeping so that I could hardly talk to her. She said, "I'm the mother of three children. I am afraid I am going to die. The doctor said so-and-so-and-so. There is no hope for me. I must leave my children and my husband."

I answered, "Whoever told you that is a liar." And that woman is sitting here in the audience today, a well woman. Beloved, she

7

might have been dead. We might have been conducting another funeral. But faith in the living God brought the confidence of power over the thing that was crushing the life out of that soul, and it went by the grace of God. No case is too hopeless.

Not a dead Jesus, but a living Christ! Not a sepulchre with a dead man in it, but the glorious, risen, present Christ in your heart and mine! The Christ lives! Not only at the right hand of God, but the Christ lives in your soul and mine, and the victory that He attained is evidenced not only by the declaration, "I am he that liveth, and was dead; and, behold, I am alive forevermore," but the victory He attains through you and me.

Bless God for the Christ who dared to enter into the very jaws of death and grapple with the enemy that no man had ever dared to tackle and He came forth the victor. He took him captive, broke his power, bound him in chains, and declared liberty to the world that was crushed and shackled by the consciousness of the power of death.

As the coming of Christ approaches, that coming which I believe a multitude of Christian hearts are looking for in these days, the flash and flame and consciousness of the Master Son of God takes possession of their hearts and minds and in the name of Jesus, men are rising up everywhere who refuse to be bound by sin and sickness and death.

That is the reason that John saw in his vision of the Revelation, a day of triumph, when all that were in earth and the sea and under, when heaven and earth are united to send forth a shout of triumph that will ring through the eternities, because the Christ of God had become the acknowledged Master, Ruler, Prince, and King of the race.

If the blessed Spirit of God keeps on revealing the mighty power of the living Christ in the souls of men, we shall have to have a new hymnbook. We shall have to have a new class of poets in the world. They used to sing dreary old hymns in the little Scotch church when I was a boy, and I remember one particular hymn:

> Hark! From the tomb a doleful sound;
> Mine ear attend the cry.
> Ye living men come view the ground,
> Where you must shortly lie.

Oh bless God for the revelation of the living Christ in the souls of men, that lifts the consciousness of men from the place of defeat into the place of power, the exultant, present, mighty power of the living God!

8

THE MIRACLE MINISTRY OF WILLIAM T. DUGAN

One Sunday afternoon a tall Englishman walked into my church in Johannesburg, South Africa. He had a top of red hair that made him as conspicuous as a lion. He walked up the aisle and took a seat quite near the front. My old preaching partner was endeavoring to explain the mighty power of the living Christ as best he could, and this man sat listening. Presently he arose, saying, "Sir, if the things you are talking about are all right, I am your candidate."

He added, "I used to be a Christian, but I came to Africa and lived the usual African life and the result is that for three years I have been unable to do anything and my physicians say I am incurable. Tell me what to do!"

My old partner asked, "John, what shall we do?" I replied, "Call him up; we shall pray for him right now." We stepped off the platform, put our hands on William T. Dugan, and instantly—as a flash of lightning blasting a tree or rock—the power of God went through the man's being, and the Lord Jesus Christ made him well.

A few days afterward he came to my house in the middle of the day and said, "Lake, I want you to show me how to get a clean heart." I took the Word of God and went through it with him to show him the mighty, cleansing, sanctifying power of the living God in a man's heart. Before he left he knelt by a chair and consecrated his life to God.

Three months passed. One day he called and said, "I have a call from God." I knew it was. There was no mistaking it. The wonder of it was in his soul. He went down into the country where a great epidemic of fever raged. Some weeks afterward I began to receive word that people were being healed. Hundreds of them! Thousands of them! One day I concluded I would go down and join in the same work a couple of hundred miles from where he was. Somehow the news traveled to him where I was, and he came there.

The next afternoon we called at the home of a man who said his wife was sick with diabetes. We prayed for the wife and several other persons who were present. Then a man stepped out into the kitchen and asked, "Would you pray for a woman like this?" When I looked at her I saw she had club feet. The right foot was on an angle of 45 degrees and the left one at right angles.

Dugan replied, "Yes. Pray for anybody." He said to her, "Sit down," and taking the club foot in his hands he said, "In the name of Jesus Christ become natural." And I want to tell you that man is in the glory presence of God today and I am going to stand there

9

with him some day. Before I had a chance to take a second breath that foot commenced to move, and the next instant that foot was straight!

Then he took up the other foot saying, "In the name of Jesus Christ become natural." Beloved, it was not the voice of the man, nor the confidence of his soul, but the mighty divine life of Jesus Christ that flashed through him and melted that foot into softness and caused it instantly to become normal by the power of God.

We have not even begun to touch the fringes of the knowledge of the power of God. However, I want to encourage your hearts: I am glad we can say what perhaps has never been said in the Christian world from the days of the apostles to the present time, that since the opening of this work in Spokane, about sixteen months ago, ten thousand people have been healed by the power of God.

CHAPTER II

The Baptism of the Holy Ghost

The outpouring of the Holy Ghost is the greatest event in Christian history—greater than the crucifixion, of greater import than the resurrection, greater than the ascension, greater than the glorification. It was the end and finality which the crucifixion, resurrection, and glorification sought to accomplish.

If Jesus Christ had been crucified and there had been no resurrection, His death on the cross would have been without avail, insofar as the salvation of mankind is concerned. Or if He had risen from the grave in resurrection, failed to reach the throne of God and receive from the Father the gift of the Holy Ghost, the purpose for which He died and for which He arose would have been missed.

There was no failure! Jesus went to the ultimate, the very throne and heart of God, and secured right out of the heavenly treasury the Almighty Spirit and poured Him forth upon the world in divine baptism; that is why we are here!

THE BIRTHDAY OF CHRISTIANITY

The day of Pentecost was the birthday of Christianity. Christianity never existed until the Holy Ghost came from heaven. The ministry of Jesus in this world was His own divine preparation of the world for His ultimate and final ministry.

The ministry of Jesus during His earth life was localized by His humanity. Localized again in that His message was only given to Israel. But the descent of the Holy Ghost brought to the souls of men a universal ministry of Jesus right from the heart of God. Heavenly contact with the eternal God in power set their nature all aflame for God, exalted their natures unto God, and made the recipient God-like.

11

HOLY GROUND

There is no subject in all the Word of God that seems to me should be approached with so much holy reverence as the subject of the baptsim of the Holy Ghost. Beloved, my heart bleeds every day of my life when I hear the flippancy which Christians use to discuss the baptism of the Holy Ghost.

When Moses entered into the presence of God at the Burning Bush, God said, "Put off thy shoes from off thy feet, for the place whereon thou standest is holy ground." How much more so when the individual comes into the presence of God, looking for the baptism of the Holy Spirit. And remember that in order to obtain this gift, Jesus lived in the world, bled on the cross, entered into the darkness of death and hell and the grave, grappled with and strangled that accursed power, came forth again, and finally ascended to heaven in order to secure it for you and me.

If there is anything under heaven that ought to secure our reverence beyond anything else in the world, it surely is the subject of the baptism of the Holy Ghost.

Supposing that Jesus were on the cross, and we were privileged today to look into His face at this hour, I wonder what the feeling of our soul would be? Suppose we were to follow today behind the weeping company that bore His dead body and laid it in the tomb, what would our feelings be? Supposing we were to meet Him as many met Him in the garden in the glory of His resurrection? Or supposing God in His goodness would let us look into that scene of scenes at the throne of God when the heavens lifted up their gates, and the Lord of glory came in? Oh, if we could, beloved, we would have a better comprehension of the baptism of the Holy Ghost.

I believe that the first essential in a real Holy Ghost church and a real Holy Ghost work is to begin to surround the baptism of the Holy Ghost with the reverence due an experience so sacred and so terribly costly.

I have been reading the remarkable story of Sadhu Sundar Singh, an Indian holy man, who renounced the world absolutely, never married, never took any part in the affairs of the world, separated himself to religious life, practiced meditation on God and the spiritual life. When Sundar Singh found the Lord Jesus he conceived the idea of becoming a Christian Sadhu. They walk from place to place. They wear no shoes; they sleep on the ground, and their lives are utterly abandoned to God.

One of the statements of Mrs. Parker, who wrote of Sundar

Singh, was to this effect: "As you approach his presence, an awe comes over the soul. It seems you are in the presence of the original Nazarene." Let us approach the Holy of Holies with a similar awe. Let us be reverential in the presence of the glorified One.

The baptism of the Holy Ghost is peculiar to the Lord Jesus: "He shall baptize you with the Holy Ghost and with fire." Jesus Christ, the glorified, must lay His hands on you and me and bestow upon us all His own nature, the outflow of God, the substance of His soul, the quality of His mind, the very being of God Himself. "Know ye not that your body is the temple of the Holy Ghost which is in you?" A temple of God, a house of God in which God lives!

A HABITATION OF GOD

Sometimes I have tried to get it clear before my soul that God was in me. I have tried to note the incoming influence and power of that pure, sweet, living Spirit, of the eternal God. I have tried to realize His presence in my spirit, in my soul, in my hands, in my feet, in my person, and in my being—the habitation of God, God equipping the soul to minister to the world, equipping the soul that he may live forever in harmony with the mind of God. For all the God-like qualities of your heart are due to the fact that God by the Spirit dwells in you.

The baptism of the Holy Ghost was the incoming of God in personality in order that the man, through this force, might be moved by God. God lives in him, speaks through him in the impulse of his soul. God has His dwelling place in him.

You may have God! That is the wonder of the baptism of the Spirit. It is not a work of grace; it is God possessing you. Oh, your heart may have been as sinful as the heart of man was ever sinful. But Christ comes to your soul. That spirit of darkness that possessed you goes and in its stead, a new spirit comes to your soul. That spirit of darkness that possessed you goes, and in its stead a new spirit comes in, the Spirit of Christ.

A TRANSFORMATION

Sin manifests itself in three ways: in thought, in acts, in nature. Salvation is a complete transformation. God takes possession of man, changes his thoughts; in consequence his acts change, his nature is new. A Christian is not a reformed man. He is a man renewed, remade by the Spirit of God, a man indwelt by God. That is the purpose and power of the baptism of the Holy Ghost.

13

When God baptizes you in the Holy Ghost, He gives you the biggest gift that heaven or earth ever possessed. He gives you Himself. He joins you by one Spirit to Himself forever.

THE REQUIREMENT

The requirement is a surrendered heart, a surrendered mind, a surrendered life. From the day that a man becomes a child of God, baptized in the Holy Ghost, it was God's intention through Jesus Christ that man should be a revelation of Jesus, not of himself any more. What do you look for in a man baptized in the Holy Ghost? You would look for a revelation of the personality of God, God moving in him, God speaking in him, through him, using his hands, his feet, a mind in harmony with God, a soul in touch with Him, a spirit united in Jesus Christ.

It is not for my heart to discourage any man, nor to make you disbelieve for one moment in the trueness of your own baptism in the Holy Ghost. I believe God by His Spirit has baptized many in the Holy Ghost. But beloved, we have not comprehended the greatness of God's intent. Not that we have not received the Spirit, but our lives have not been sufficiently surrendered to God. We must keep on ascending right to the throne, right to the heart of God, right into the soul of the glorified.

THE HOLY GHOST NOT A GIFT OF POWER, BUT OF GOD HIMSELF

The common teaching that my heart these days is endeavoring to combat is that God comes to present the individual with a gift of power, and the individual is then supposed to go out and manifest some certain characteristic of power. No! God comes to present you with Himself. "Ye shall receive power after that the Holy Ghost is come upon you."

Jesus went to heaven in order that the very treasury of the heart of the eternal God might be unlocked for your benefit and that out of the very soul of the eternal God, the streams of His life and nature would possess you from the crown of your head to the sole of your feet. He went, that there would be just as much of the eternal God in your hands, feet, and in your brain as each is capable of containing.

In other words, from the very soles of our feet to the last hair on top of your head, every cell of your being would be a residence of the Spirit of the living God. In the truest sense man is the dwelling place of God, the house of God, the tabernacle of the Most High.

How trifling are the controversies that surround the baptism of the Holy Ghost. Men are debating such trifling issues. For instance, does a man speak in tongues, or does he not? Do not think for a moment that I am discounting the value of tongues. I am not. But beloved, I will tell you for what my heart is straining. At Jerusalem they not only spoke in tongues, but they spoke in the languages of the nations. If it was possible for Peter and Paul, then it is possible for every last one not to speak in tongues alone, as we ordinarily understand that phrase, but to speak because God dwells in you in other languages. And if our present experience in tongues is not satisfying, God bless you, go on into languages, as God meant that you should.

The unknown tongue of the Spirit was to teach you of God, to be a faith builder in your soul, to take you out into God's big practical endeavor to save the world. And that is the reason, dear ones, that I want to bring this issue to your soul. In the matter of the baptism of the Holy Spirit, we are in a state of the merest infancy of understanding, the merest infancy of divine control, the merest infancy in ability to assimilate our environment, including the full meaning of speaking in other tongues.

A weak Christianity always wants to drop to the imperfect and adjust itself to the popular mind. But a real Christianity seeks to be made perfect in God, both in character and gifts.

MY PERSONAL EXPERIENCE

Dear ones, I want to repeat a little of my own personal history on the subject of the baptism of the Spirit.

I knelt under a tree when about sixteen years of age in repentance and prayer, and God came into my soul. I was saved from my sins, and from that day I knew Jesus Christ a living Saviour. There never was a single moment of question about the reality of His coming into my life as a Saviour, for He saved me from my sins. My friends said, "You are baptized in the Holy Ghost."

Some time later, I think when I was yet under twenty, I met a Christian farmer, Melvin Pratt, who sat down on his plow handles and taught me the subject of sanctification, and God let me enter into that experience. My friends said, "Now, you surely are baptized in the Holy Ghost."

Later in my life I came under the ministry of George G. Watson of the Christian and Missionary Alliance, who taught me with more clearness and better distinction between the baptism of the Holy Ghost and sanctification, and I entered into a richer life and a better experience. A beautiful anointing of the Spirit was upon my life.

Then the ministry of healing was opened to me, and I ministered for ten years in the power of God. Hundreds and hundreds of people were healed by the power of God during this ten years, and I could feel the conscious flow of the Holy Spirit through my soul and my hands.

But at the end of that ten years I believe I was the hungriest man for God that ever lived. There was such a hunger for God that as I left my offices in Chicago and walked down the street, my soul would break out and I would cry, "Oh God!" I have had people stop and look at me and wonder. It was the yearning passion of my soul, asking for God in a greater measure than I knew.

But my friends would say, "Mr. Lake, you have a beautiful baptism in the Holy Ghost." Yes, it was nice as far as it went, but it was not answering the cry of my heart. I was growing up into a larger understanding of God and my own soul's need. My soul was demanding a greater entrance into God, His love, presence, and power.

MY BAPTISM IN THE HOLY GHOST

And then one day an old man strolled into my office, sat down, and in the next half hour he revealed more of the knowledge of God to my soul than I had ever known before. When he left I said, "God bless that old grey head. That man knows more of God than any man I ever met. By the grace of God, if that is what the baptism of the Holy Ghost with tongues does, I am going to possess it." Oh the wonder of God that was then revealed to my heart!

I went into fasting and prayer and waiting on God for nine months. And one day the glory of God in a new manifestation and a new incoming came to my life. When the phenomena had passed and the glory of it remained in my soul, I found that my life began to manifest in the varied range of the gifts of the Spirit. I spoke in tongues by the power of God, and God flowed through me with a new force. Healings were of a more powerful order. Oh, God lived in me; God manifested in me; God spoke through me. My spirit was deified; I had a new comprehension of God's will, a new discernment of spirit, a new revelation of God in me.

16

THE DISCERNING OF DISEASES

Then a new wonder manifested. My nature became so sensitized that I could lay hands on any man or woman and tell what organ was diseased, and to what extent, and all about it. I tested it. I went into hospitals where physicians could not diagnose a case, touched a patient and instantly I knew the organ that was diseased, its extent, condition, and location. And one day it passed away. A child plays with a toy, and his joy is so wonderful he sometimes forgets to eat.

Don't you remember when you first were baptized in the Holy Ghost and you first spoke in tongues, how you bubbled and babbled —it was so wonderful, so amazing? We just wanted to be babies and go on bubbling and exhilarating. And now we are wondering what is the matter. The effervescence seems to have passed away. My! It is a good thing for you that it did. God is letting your soul down, beloved, into the bedrock, right down where your mind is not occupied any more with the manifestation of God. God is trying to get your mind occupied with Himself. God has come into you and He is drawing you into Himself.

Will you speak in tongues when you are baptized in the Holy Ghost? Yes, you will (if you received that standard of baptism), but you will do an awful lot more than that, bless God. You will speak with the soul of Jesus Christ. You will feel with the heart of the Son of God. Your pulse will beat with a heavenly desire to bless the world, because it is the pulse of Jesus that is throbbing in your soul. And I do not believe there will be a bit of inclination in your heart to turn around to another child of God and say, "You are not in my class. I am baptized in the Holy Ghost."

That is as foreign to the Spirit of the Son of God as night is from day. Beloved, if you are baptized in the Holy Ghost there will be a tenderness in your soul so deep that you will never crush the aspiration of another heart by a single suggestion, but your soul will throb and beat and pulse in love, and your heart will be under that one to lift it up to God and push it out as far into the glory as your faith can send it.

I want to talk with the utmost frankness and say to you that tongues have been to me the making of my ministry. It is that peculiar communication with God when God reveals to my soul the truth I utter to you day by day in my ministry. But that time of communication with me is mostly in the night. Many a time I climb out of bed, take my pencil and pad, and jot down the beautiful things of God, the wonderful things of God that He talks out in my spirit, reveals to my heart.

17

THE LANGUAGE OF THE SPIRIT

The spirit of man has a voice. Do you get that? The spirit of man has a voice. The action of God in your spirit causes your spirit to speak by its voice. In order to make it intelligent to your understanding it has to be repeated to you in the language that your brain knows. Why? Because there is a language common to the spirit of man; it is not English; it is not German; it is not French; it is not Italian, nor any of the other languages of the earth. It is a language of the spirit of man. And oh what a joy it was when that pent-up, bursting, struggling spirit of yours found its voice and "spake in tongues"!

Many a time I have talked to others in the Spirit, by the Spirit, through the medium of tongues and knew everything that was said to me, but I did not know it with this ear. It was not the sound of their words. It was that indefinable something that makes it intelligent. Spirit speaks to spirit, just as mouth speaks to mouth, or as man speaks to man. Your spirit speaks to God. God is Spirit. He answers back. Bless God.

INTERNAL REVELATION MADE INTELLIGENT BY INTERPRETATION

But if you want to make that medium of internal revelation of God intelligent to other folks, then it must be translated into the language that they know. That is the reason the apostle said, "Let him that speaketh in an unknown tongue pray that he may interpret," that the church may receive edifying. Paul says, "In the church I had rather speak five words with my understanding, that by my voice I might teach others also, than ten thousand words in an unknown tongue." Your revelation from God is given you in tongues, but you give it forth in the language the people understand.

Beloved, settle it. It is one of the divine mediums and methods of communication between your spirit and God's. And as long as you live, when you talk about tongues, speak with reverence, for it is God. When you talk about healing, speak with reverence, for it is God. When you talk about prophecy, remember it is God.

Tongues are for a sign, not to them that believe, but to them that believe not. But prophecy, the outspeaking for God, is for all. Therefore, Paul does not want us to crush a man who is speaking in tongues, but to keep our hands off and stand back. Leave him

18

alone with God. Let him go out into the tongues of God. Let him travel away out in His love and power and come back with messages to his soul.

However, he must not monopolize the time of hundreds of people in the church with a private communication of God to his soul. But when he has completed his interview with God, he gives forth his knowledge as interpretation or prophecy.

There have been so many controversies over the various gifts of the Spirit as they have appeared one after another. Twenty-five or thirty years ago when we began in the ministry of healing, we had a fight to keep from being submerged by our opposing brethren in Jesus Christ who thought one was insane because he suggested that the Lord Jesus Christ could still heal. In the state of Michigan I had to go into the courts to keep some of my friends out of the insane asylum, because they believed God could not heal without pills or some other material aids.

It was simply that they did not understand the eternal and invisible nature of God. They had no idea God could be ministered through a man's hands and soul, fill a sick man's body, take possession of and make him whole. The world has had to learn this fact. It is a science far in advance of so-called material or physical science.

THE COMING REVIVAL

The marvelous wave of God came over the country from 1900 to 1906 when hundreds of thousands of people were baptized in the Holy Ghost and spoke in tongues. But listen! John Alexander Dowie, riding on the wave of that wonderful manifestation of healing power, wanted to build a church and stamp it with healing only, and his church practically did that, and died. Other churches branded theirs with holiness only and died. Others advocated an anointing of the Holy Ghost called "baptism," and they died in power also.

Later on we wanted to build a great structure and stamp it with tongues. And after a while the tongues got dry. Somehow the glory and the glow had gone out of them. They became rattly and did not sound right. What was the matter? Nothing was wrong with the experience. God had not departed from the life, but was hidden from our view. We were absorbed in the phenomena of God, not in God Himself. Now we must go on!

I can see as my spirit discerns the future and reaches out to

19

touch the heart of mankind and the desire of God, that there is coming from heaven a new manifestation of the Holy Ghost in power, and that new manifestations will be in sweetness, in love, in tenderness, in the power of the Spirit, beyond anything your heart or mine ever saw. The very lightning of God will flash through men's souls. The sons of God will meet the sons of darkness and prevail. Jesus Christ will destroy the antichrist.

A DELUGE OF THE SPIRIT IN AFRICA

In 1908 I preached at Pretoria, South Africa, when one night God came over my life in such power, in such streams of liquid glory and power that it flowed consciously off my hands like streams of electricity. I could point my finger at a man, and that stream would strike him. When a man interrupted the meeting, I pointed my finger at him and said, "Sit down!" He fell as if struck, and lay for three hours. When he became normal, they asked him what had happened, and he said, "Something struck me that went straight through me. I thought I was shot."

At two o'clock in the morning I ministered to sixty-five sick who were present, and the streams of God that were pouring through my hands were so powerful, the people would fall as though they were hit. I was troubled when they fell with such violence. And the Spirit said, "You do not need to put your hands on them. Keep your hands a distance away." And when I held my hands a foot from their heads, they would crumple and fall in a heap on the floor. They were healed almost every one.

That was the outward manifestation. That was what the people saw. But beloved, something transpired in my heart that made my soul like the soul of Jesus Christ. Oh, there was a tenderness, a newborn tenderness of God that was so wonderful that my heart reached out and cried and wept over men in sin. I would gather them in my arms and love them, and Jesus Christ flowed out of me and delivered them.

During that period men would walk down the aisle, and when they came within ten feet of me, I have seen them fall prostrate, one on top of another. A preacher who had sinned, as he looked at me fell prostrate, was saved, baptized in the Holy Ghost, and stirred the nation with his message of love.

In eighteen months God raised up one hundred churches in the land. Those hundred churches were born in my tabernacle at Johannesburg. The multitude of those who composed these hundred churches were healed or baptized in the Holy Ghost under my own eyes as I preached or prayed.

I continued in the ministry of healing until I saw hundreds of thousands healed. All the time my heart kept saying, "Oh God, let me know you better. I want you; my heart wants you too, God." There was a cry in my soul for a greater consciousness of God, a yearning for Christ's own life and love.

I shall never forget Spokane, Washington, for during the first six months I was there, God satisfied the cry of my heart. God came in and my mind opened, and my spirit understood afresh. I was able to tell of God and talk out of my heart of God as I had never been able to before. God reached a new depth in my spirit and revealed new possibilities in God.

So beloved, you pray through. Pray through for your church, pray through for your work. Oh, God will come! God will come with power greater than your eyes ever beheld. God will come with waves of heavenly love and sweetness and blessed be God, your heart will be satisfied with Him.

How are you going to get Him? Oh, I would abandon my soul. I would abandon my soul to God. Oh, I would discard the selfishness of the world. When a man enters into Jesus Christ, he enters into life anew.

The greatest manifestation of the Holy Ghost baptized life ever given to the world was not in the preaching of the apostles; it was not in the wonderful manifestations of God that took place at their hands. It was in the unselfishness manifested by the church. Think of it! Three thousand Holy Ghost baptized Christians in Jerusalem from the day of Pentecost onward who loved their neighbors' children as much as their own, who were so anxious for fear their brethren did not have enough to eat, that they sold their estates, brought the money, laid it at the apostles' feet and said, "Distribute it. Carry the glow and the fire and the wonder of this divine salvation to the whole world." That showed what God had wrought in their hearts. Oh, I wish we could arrive at that place, where this church were baptized to that degree of unselfishness.

That would be a greater manifestation than healing, greater than conversion, greater than baptism in the Holy Ghost, greater than tongues. It would be a manifestation of the love of I Corinthians 13 that so many preach about and do not possess. When a man sells his all for God and distributes it for the kingdom's good, it will speak louder of love than the evangelists who harp about love and oppose tongues and the other gifts of the Spirit.

21

That was the same Holy Ghost that came upon the disciples and caused them to speak in tongues. No more grabbing for themselves. No more bantering for the biggest possible salary, no more juggling to put themselves and their friends in the most influential positions. All the old characteristics were gone. They were truly saved. Why their hearts were like the heart of Jesus; their soul was like the soul of God. They loved as God loved; they loved the world; they loved sinners so that they gave their all to save them.

Do you want Him? You can have Him. Oh, He will come and fill your soul. Oh, the Holy Ghost will take possession of your life. He will reveal the wonder of heaven, the glory of God, the richness and purity of His holiness and make you sweet and God-like forever.

CHAPTER III

The Spirit of Apostleship and the Spirit of Real Christianity

(Preached at an Ordination Service)

I want to discuss the spirit of apostleship and the spirit of real Christianity with you today. People fail to see that Jesus Christ laid the underlying structure that made the church a possibility. Have you ever stopped to think where the timber came from that kept the apostolic board filled as one after another was martyred?

Very few Christians are aware of that fact, that Jesus provided not only the twelve apostles, but He provided "seventy other also." And while the twelve walked with Him and talked with Him and were His immediate companions and inner circle, after the crucifixion of Jesus as one or another departed from the board of the twelve, their place was filled out of the seventy.

THE MINISTRY OF THE SEVENTY

Matthias was one of the seventy. Hippolytus of the early Christian fathers, who wrote about 300 years after Jesus Christ, gives the names of the seventy. And it will be astonishing to take your Bibles and discover that the New Testament speaks of thirty-two of the seventy. In one single verse in Romans, Paul names five of them.

If one happened to occupy the position of apostle it was not because he was strutting around as a self-important official. It was because necessity demanded it. As Paul said where he wrote with dignity and strength and power to the church: "Paul, an apostle of Jesus Christ (not by the will of man but) by the will of God," that his words might come to the multitudes with that due strength that weight and power that brought conviction to their hearts and helped them to realize that as the mouthpiece of God he was speaking God's Word, and God's final Word.

Then there were also bishops. No doubt many a Christian has wondered who Ananias was, who laid his hands on Paul that he might receive the Holy Ghost. Hippolytus tells us that Ananias

23

was bishop of Damascus, one of the seventy appointed by Jesus.

Barnabas was the companion of Paul, was also one of the seventy, and was bishop of Milan. Aristobulus, appointed by Jesus as one of the seventy was bishop to Britain. I wish we knew more about Aristobulus. I would like to be acquainted with the character of the man that brought the Gospel of the Son of God to the British Isles.

It suffices us to say that the New Testament speaks of twenty-one apostles, not twelve. Matthias was the thirteenth, Paul and Barnabas were the fourteenth and fifteenth. Apollos was the sixteenth. Andronicus and Justus are distinguished by Paul with this statement that they were chief men among the apostles. They were men of unusual force and power of wise counsel. There were others.

APOSTLES' CHARACTER

I am interested in what constitutes the character of an apostle. The modern conception of an apostle is usually that he is a big church boss, but that was not the conception Jesus left. He took the twelve aside just before His departure, took a basin in His hand, tied a towel around His waist, knelt down and washed the feet of the lot of them, and when He finished He said to them, "If I then, your Lord and Master, have washed your feet, ye also ought to wash one another's feet."

An apostle was not to be a big boss; he was to be like his Lord — a servant of all. Oh, I like that democratic spirit of the New Testament that leaves off the titles but looks into the face of a man's soul and identifies him as Peter and as John and Apollos and all the rest. When we come down the line of twenty-one apostles, we find among other things that fourteen out of twenty-one gave their lives for the gospel of Jesus Christ. Five of them gave their lives on olive trees, where they did not take time to make crosses, but nailed them to the first thing that they could find. Thomas died in India being pierced through both ways and left to die. That is the character of apostleship; that is the character of Christianity.

That is the reason that before His arrest after He had eaten with them, He took the cup and when He had drunk said: "The new testament in my blood." The thing that gave it significance was the pledge that was made. From time immemorial men have pledged themselves under every circumstance. The old Romans, before a great battle were in the habit of gathering together, while the commander took the cup in his hands, to drink to the pledge that they all gave for the honor of Rome and that they would never retreat. That is what gave them their invincible character and that carried their conquest throughout the world.

Jesus Christ was not behind that conception in His endeavor to put that spirit of God and fidelity in the soul of Christianity. He called the twelve together, stood before them, and taking the cup in His hands said in their presence, "The new testament in my blood." And when He had drunk, He gave it to Peter and handed it to John, and to each one in his turn. And when they had drunk with the Son of God, accepting that pledge, it meant to Peter, "The new testament in my blood," and it meant the same to James and to Andrew. And to every one of them in their soul they gave assent to the pledge of Jesus, "The new testament in my blood."

That is the conquering spirit of apostleship in Jesus Christ, that conquering spirit of Christianity born out of the soul of the Son of God. That is the reason that Christians look to their Lord, not as a coward, not quailing from suffering and hiding in fear, but they look to Him as the boldest of the bold, as He dared to do what never man dared.

Who can help but love that character of a Christian? And beloved you who have listened to my voice for six or seven years past know that my heart has asked, my soul has cried, and my nature has longed that God might bring forth in this city a Christian character of that order that will stand forever as a divine monument of eternal faithfulness and fidelity in Jesus Christ to the truths of the Son of God.

Yes, I have confidence in you. Other souls may shatter on the rocks; other souls may wither in disappointment, but the lives that have been planted in that spirit of divine fidelity to Jesus Christ are unconquerable. They will triumph in the world. In the midst of the sentiment of modern church life, the world is waiting for those who dare again to walk out on the platform of the Son of God and stand there, bless God!

That is the reason that by the grace of God we take our place by the side of the Son of God and without dodging we endeavor to accept the platform on which our Lord has stood. "The Spirit of the Lord," said Jesus, "is upon me; because he hath anointed me to preach the gospel to the poor; he hath sent me to heal the brokenhearted, to preach deliverance to the captives, and recovering of sight to the blind, to set at liberty them that are bruised, to preach the acceptable year of the Lord."

Not the everlasting waiting for the year of the jubilee—no sir!

Jesus Christ had come, the eternal jubilee, everlastingly available. He was at hand. Come in and take the blessing and by the grace of God enjoy the benediction of heaven that the Christ has provided.

My heart has ever coveted one thing above everything else; and that is that I might have been one of the company who sat with Jesus that night and might have taken the cup from His hands and drunk it like a man, saying, "The new testament in my blood." I bless God that throughout the ages, Jesus Christ has left a chosen church and a chosen generation of men and women who love the Lord, who can take the cup in their hands, and who can drink His blood again, declaring as He did, "The new testament in my blood," and live it and die by it!

TESTED IN SOUTH AFRICA

One day some years ago, being environed by certain conditions powerful and influential enemies who pamphleteered us throughout the whole world, broke confidence in our work for God to that extent that the little pittance of financial support almost dwindled away. I had one hundred and twenty workers out on the frontiers of South Africa, beyond the confines of civilization. The question arose as to what to do for these at such an hour. I said, "There is only one thing. That is, be honorable with these men and women. Let them know the true condition. If possible, let us call them in and let them decide as to the best thing to do."

So we sold our household possessions; we sold our watches, we sold everything that was salable for money enough to bring that hundred and twenty in. When they arrived in Johannesburg, I poured my heart out to them as I am to you today. And after a while they said, "Brother Lake, we would like to be alone for a little while and we ask you to retire. We have a decision to make."

I retired into the vestry for a half hour, and then they called me in. When I came in I found the hundred and twenty sitting in an oval in the middle of the tabernacle. They had cleared the chairs away, made a large open circle with a hundred and twenty seats around, and a little table in the middle with bread and wine. They said, "Brother Lake, we have made our decision. We are going back to our fields. If we die, if our wives die, if our children die, we will never reduce that ministry that Jesus Christ has established through this work in Africa."

They said, "Brother Lake, serve the bread and wine." I took my place at the head of the circle and started the bread around and the wine around. And every man said, "The new testament in my blood," meaning "my blood to save South Africa."

They put only one restriction: They said, "Brother, if we die, one request—come and bury us." And twelve times in that year of hell, I stood beside twelve of the finest men and sixteen of the finest women and children God ever let live in this world. I buried them because they starved to death, or they died because they could not get proper nourishment, such as a white man could live on.

That is the reason that the work in South Africa lives, and that is the reason that all the damnation on earth has never been able to assail it. But like a conquering glory it has gone on these years, conquering and conquering in the name of our Christ, until my hundred and twenty have grown to two hundred and fifty white preachers of the same character and until our five hundred black preachers have grown to be twelve hundred preachers of the same type and character, and until our mission stations are planted all over Southern Africa.

When I left Spokane a year and a half ago, I asked, "Lord Jesus, have I failed to put that spirit in the souls of this people here? After living in it and being one of it, have I failed in this land of of light and love and plenty to put that spirit of Jesus in the souls of my own people? But bless God when I came back this time, I have a new feeling in my heart. I can say to my Christ, 'Lord, it is there. Bless God it is there!' "

All the heroes of Jesus did not live in the first century, nor in the fourth century. They live today! No sir! If I were compelled to ordain men and women to the Gospel of Jesus Christ and then feel that I only had a lot of weaklings on my hands I would apologize to Jesus Christ and quit the business.

But I want to say, my soul has touched the soul of this people. My heart has felt a new lift in God, a new response from the depth of this city, and I know today there is faithfulness to Jesus Christ in this people that is unsurpassed in the world. I call on you in the name of the Lord Jesus Christ to let it come forth in your life.

Some of the early Christians thought they were having a hard time, and they wrote complaining to the apostle. He was not very comforting. It reminded me of a missionary I once had. I was in Los Angeles, and he wrote me from the heart of Basutoland. He said, "Mr. Lake, the soles are worn out of my shoes, and my feet are bleeding, my shins are cut, and my body is sore." I guess the

27

poor boy felt he needed a little sympathy, but he did not get it. I wrote back, "Brother, your shoes are worn-out and your feet are bleeding for the Lord Jesus Christ. Men's feet have bled and their body is sore in the service of the devil many a time, and surely we can go just as far, and a little farther for the Son of God and eternal life."

I bless God for these years in Spokane. People think our life has been stormy, but to me it has been a practical quiet, and somehow I feel the old stirring. I feel once again a passion, a yearning in my heart for a world away from God, that once lifted my soul into the heavenlies and gave me the driving force to accomplish for Him.

But I must bring this talk to a close, for we have a sacred ceremony to perform. We purpose this afternoon to ordain a group of men and women as elders in the church.

PRAYER

God, my heavenly Father, how I pray today that that same pure spirit of Jesus Christ from heaven that burned in the hearts of Peter and John and Paul, and that carried them over the mountains through the deserts and over burning sands in the midst of assassins. betrayed by false brethren, and every other character of evil and led them victoriously will come to our souls.

Lord God, we ask thee by thy grace this day, to make it so. Lord let it be so, and our faith claims it, that everyone this afternoon upon whom hands shall be laid, and this church, dear God, shall come forth and rededicate themselves to this blessed life, this holy effort for mankind.

CHAPTER IV

The Power of Divine Healing

My soul used to be able to enjoy just as much lightness in the Lord Jesus as anybody, but the various processes of life reduced my capacity to enjoy jingles, and God brought me down to the solids of life. No man can live in the environment in which a large portion of my life has been spent without realizing that unless men contact God in real power, power out of the ordinary, power sufficient for tremendous needs and unusual occasions, they cannot live.

DOMINION OVER A FEVER EPIDEMIC

In South Africa some years ago in a single night a fever epidemic struck the country for three hundred and fifty miles. As I rode through a section of that area, I found men dead in their beds beside their wives; children dead in their beds alongside the living: whole families stricken, dying, and some dead. In one single month one-fourth of the entire population of that district, both white and black died. We had to organize an army to dig graves and an army of men to make caskets. We could not buy wood enough in that section of the country to make caskets, so we buried them in a blanket, or without a blanket, when it was necessary to save the blankets for a better purpose.

I had a man in my company whom God anointed to pray as I never found anybody else anointed to pray. For days he remained under a thorn tree, and when I passed in the morning I would hear his voice in prayer, and when I returned in the evening I would hear his voice in prayer. Many times I got a prepared meal and carried it to him and aroused him long enough to get him to eat it. I would ask, "Brother, how is it? Are you getting through?" He would reply, "Not yet." But one day he said: "Mr. Lake, I feel today that if I had just a little help in faith that my spirit would go through to God." And I went on my knees beside him, joined my heart with his, and voiced my prayer to God.

As we prayed, the Spirit of the Lord overwhelmed our souls and presently I found myself, not kneeling under the tree, but moving

29

gradually away from the tree, some fifty or one hundred feet. My eyes gradually opened, and I witnessed such a scene as I never witnessed before—a multitude of demons like a flock of sheep! The Spirit had come upon him also, and he rushed ahead of me, cursing that army of demons, and they were driven back to hell, or the place from whence they came. Beloved, the next morning when we awoke, that epidemic of fever was gone. That is the power of divine healing — God destroying Satan.

Now when you consider that I have been a man of some scientific training, you can understand what an introduction into a life meant where everything was made new and of a different order. Instead of being on the hard, natural plane of materialistic life and knowledge, now suddenly introduced into the Spirit, you can realize what a revolution was brought to pass in my soul, and how gradually discovery after discovery revealed the wonder of God and the mighty action of God through the souls of men.

THE INTERACTION OF FAITH AND THE SPIRIT

There is a little keynote in one of Paul's epistles that gives the real key to victorious prayer. In successful prayer there is divine action, a divine interpretation, an interaction just as real as any chemical interaction in any scientific experiment.

So it is in the spiritual realm. Paul gave us this key: "The word . . . did not profit them, not being mixed with faith." There is a quality in the soul of man, a necessary quality which is faith. In the soul of God is another quality. That quality is the power of the Spirit. And when faith and the Spirit come together, there is an interaction. There is a movement of God. There is a manifestation of the Spirit. There is a divine explosion! Faith and God united is divine healing.

When I was a boy, a neighbor employed a chemist. They were trying to manufacture a new explosive of some kind. A section of the barn was used for the experiments. Johnny was strictly reminded that he had no business around the barn, but like many boys his curiosity was aroused. One day when they had gone to town he discovered the door was not thoroughly locked. With just a little picking and prying it opened, and Johnny was inside. There were some packages on the bench and some liquid on the floor. Presently Johnny bungled; a package fell into the bucket of liquid, and that is the last that Johnny remembered. When he came to himself he was some distance away, carried on a section of wall. The package in the liquid had interacted.

One can imagine somewhat of the terrific energy stored up in a block of nitroglycerine. But when you come to think of the marvel of the nature of God, the dynamics of His being, how staggering His Almightiness becomes! The world's conception of religion is that it is a matter of sentiment. To them it is not a thing of power, and they do not understand the properties of the soul of God, nor the quality of His life, nor how it is that God moves in the nature of men to change their heart, to dissolve the sin out of their soul, to cleanse them by His life and power, to heal their body and reveal His light, life, and nature in them.

I believe the very beautiful thing we call salvation and the holy statement of Jesus Christ, "Ye must be born again," is itself a scientific fact, and a declaration of God's divine purpose and intent, based on the law of being.

I want to tell you beloved that there is a process in a man's soul that admits God into his life. Your heart opens because it is touched by the love of God, and into the heart, into the nature of man there comes the divine essence of the living Spirit, and bless God it has an action in him. Sin dissolves from his nature and from the mind of man. The Spirit of God takes possession of the cells of his brain, and his thoughts are changed by his action. There is a new realization of divine holiness.

Beloved, Jesus Christ had His eye and His soul fixed on that one dynamic power of God, the Holy Ghost. And His life, His death, His resurrection, His ascension to glory were all necessary before He arrived at the throne of God where He could receive from the Father the gift of the Holy Ghost and have the privilege of ministering it to your soul and mine.

So in my heart there has grown a wondrous reverence for the mighty Son of God, who saw beyond the kin of man, who visioned in the distance, who sought in His soul for the key to the mighty powers of the nature of God, who determined for our benefit and salvation to leave the throne of glory, come to earth, be born as a man, and take upon Him the naure of man. He looked to God as men do, overcame by His power through reliance on His Word, and so believing, so advancing step by step in the nature of God and the likeness of God, one day He stood forth, the Eternal Sacrifice before the throne of God and received the eternal reward of His fidelity—the Holy Ghost. In life, Jesus the man was the likeness of God; in resurrection, the nature of God; in glorification the substance of God and author of eternal salvation.

DIVINE TRANSMUTATION

There is a process of divine transmutation. The old alchemists searched through the ages for the process by which the baser metals could be transformed into gold. But beloved by the power of God's Spirit in a man's heart, that process is going on every single day of your life, wherein God takes that which is earthly, touches it by His divine power, moves upon it by His mighty Spirit, regenerates it by His heavenly nature and in the name of Jesus Christ you come forth no longer self and selfish, but now transmuted, changed by the power of Christ into the nature of the Son of God, into the likeness of the Lord, into His character, nature, understanding and knowledge.

By these we become "partakers of the divine nature," and in consequence, "escape the corruption that is in the world through lust." His divine purpose is not to whitewash the soul, but to change the character, transmute the life by the grace of God, make the man a king, a deliverer in common with the Lord Jesus Christ his elder Brother. If I am a brother of the Lord's then I am bone of His bone, flesh of His flesh, and substance of His substance, like my elder brother. The source of life is the same source of life that is in Him, the same purpose that is revealed in Him in His high purpose for you and for me.

Men have little understanding of the quality of faith or what it accomplishes, because of the fact that they are not aware of the process by which that work is done. Faith has the quality and power with the Spirit of God, to do what a match does to powder. It is the touch of God. It is the touch of faith through us that ignites the Spirit and produces the divine action that takes place in the soul, where sin is rebuked and cast out, when sickness is destroyed and dissolved from the life. The nature is set free, and man rejoices as a son of God—saved in spirit, soul, and body.

A CHILD'S FAITH

One day there came to my healing rooms a little boy that we know on the streets as a newsboy, just as one of the little ragged chaps. A lady had observed the little fellow fall on the street in an epileptic fit; afterwards we took him by the hand and led him to the healing rooms. We talked to the little chap about the Lord, prayed for him, and told him to return again. The Lord healed him. He was a manly little urchin, and one day he said, "Mr. Lake,

I haven't any money to reward you with now, but you are not going to lose any money on me." We smiled and were glad to see the spirit of the little chap, and he went his way. About two weeks later in the midst of a great meeting, he strutted in, marched up, and laid five silver dollars on the table, and marched out again.

Then he came up against his first real problem of living his new life in his business. Every boy has a corner. He can sell papers on his own corner, and it is up to him to keep all other boys away, but now he had given his heart to the Lord. One day he came around with a long face. He said, "It's all off."

"Well, my boy, what is the trouble?"

"They were just going to rush my corner, until I could not stand it, and I cleaned up the whole bunch." The little chap was getting his first introduction into the real problem of being a Christian in this old world under a competitive system, the outgrowth of human selfishness devised by the devil.

One day a gentleman came along and wanted to buy a paper. His arm was disabled, and he could not get his purse. He said to the boy, "I have put my purse in the wrong pocket. Put your hand in and get it for me." The boy asked, "What is the matter with your arm?"

He replied, "I have what is called neuritis. My arm is paralyzed."

The little chap said, "Well, if the doctors can't do any good, I'll tell you where you can get fixed up. There are some men up in the Rookery building that pray and get folks well."

The man asked, "How do you know?"

He replied, "I used to take fits, and fall on the street, and they would carry me off to the police station. I was like that for four years, but I don't take fits any more. If you want me to, I will take you up there."

So he brought him up. He was the head of a great lumber concern. His name was Rose. He sat down and told me how he was moved by the child's simple words, but that he had no more idea of how God could heal a man or save a man from sin than one of the Indians. So we had to begin to tell of the Lord Jesus and His power to save, and we continued to minister to him each day. Three weeks afterward, he returned again to the same medical clinic, where two hundred and seventy-five physicians had declared four weeks before that they could do nothing for him. They reexamined him and found him perfectly well, healed by the power of God. That is the power of divine healing!

I went to the Medical Association and secured a copy of the lecture that was given by Dr. Demple on the seriousness of the disease, the utter impossibility of medicine ever to help him or to change his condition. In so far as they were concerned, he was a cripple. The nerves were dead, atrophied. "It would require a miracle," they said, "to produce the original life and restore power in the tissue of the arm." But the miracle took place, because there is a Fountain of Life, the Life of God, available for every man. Bless His Name! That is the power of divine healing!

Oh, there is a negative thing, and that negative thing in religious life is what is killing the real power of God. That negative thing, when we are all the time *not* doing this and that. It is a religion of "Don't do this," and "Don't do that." When Christ comes into the soul and into the spirit, it is all changed! Instead of deadness, there is *life* in God. Instead of inaction, there is power by the Spirit of God. The Christian is a *positive* man.

I am looking to God for some real finished products these days, real men growing up in the Lord Jesus Christ, established by the splendid solidity of His holy nature and divine character, beautified by His holy glory, enriched by His divine nature—like the Son of God.

So my brother, my sister, I want to bring your heart today into this blessed confidence, this holy truth, this divine reality. If religious life has been a sort of sentiment, let me tell you that beyond it there is the power of God, the moving, dynamic, burning force of life in Jesus Christ—waiting to come into your heart, to revitalize your thought, change your spirit, and indwell the very flesh, bone, and blood of you, and make you a new man, a new woman in the Lord Jesus. Say, beloved, that is the power of divine healing!

I want to bring home the truth of God. In the minds and lives of many, religion is simply an illusion. There is no divine reality in it. But, beloved, real religion is God's divine reality, for it is the heart of God and the life of Christ. And when it comes into the soul of man it generates the same divine reality and heavenly power in him, and man becomes God's new creature.

A MIGHTY MIRACLE OF HEALING

In my younger days, when I first touched the ministry of healing, and as yet had developed a very small portion of faith in God, a young lady who lived nine miles in the country had a tubercular limb. Her physicians had tried to build up her strength so that they could amputate the limb, but on final examination the disease was found to have made such progress that the amputation would not save her life. One day we received a request to join in prayer for her the next morning at nine and to invite all the people who knew God and had faith in Him to unite with us. So I telegraphed all around the country to those I knew.

The physician told me that the knee had become so decayed that he could put his finger through the joint. Her suffering was more than ordinary. It required three men to hold her in a bed the night before she was healed.

But in the morning she desired to be left alone for the last half hour before prayer. She lay with her eyes closed and her body still, and after a while she said, "I opened my eyes and saw it was just exactly the time for the people to pray for me." She said in her soul, "It is the time I ought to be healed." So letting her faith reach out to God, she said, "In the Name of Jesus it is the time I AM healed." She made a motion toward the side of the bed, and landed out on the floor, perfectly whole. She rushed down the stairs two steps at a time. Her sister-in-law had a tub of water on the floor. She stuck her diseased limb into it, and the entire mass of rotten flesh of the leg disappeared in the tub, and there was a new leg, as new as a newly born baby, both flesh and blood and bone. That is the power of divine healing!

I traveled to Chicago and met old John Alexander Dowie, and I told him of the miracle. He asked, "Do you know the facts in this case?" I replied, "I do."

"I want to see the woman." He handed me one hundred dollars and I wired for her to come. Beloved, even in that man's life he had never realized the creative power of God. He had seen wonderful healings, but here was the *creative* action of God, instantly making muscle and bones and flesh by God's power.

Beloved, may every one of these holy demonstrations work out in your life, as they worked out in mine, a divine consciousness that God by the Spirit never comes to a man's life to whitewash him, or smooth him over, but God comes to him to make him new and give him a new heart, a new mind, a new spirit, new blood, new bone. new flesh, to send him out with a new song in his mouth, a new shout of praise in his heart, and a new realization of holiness—a truly redeemed man.

CHAPTER V

The Law of the Spirit of Life

"There is therefore now no condemnation to them which are in Christ Jesus, who walk not after the flesh, but after the Spirit. For the law of the Spirit of life in Christ Jesus hath made me free from the law of sin and death. For what the law could not do, in that it was weak through the flesh, God sending his own Son in the likeness of sinful flesh, and for sin, condemned sin in the flesh" (Romans 8:1-3).

For a long time I wondered what these two expressions meant— "sin in the flesh," and "the law of the Spirit of life in Christ Jesus . . . made me free from the law of sin and death."

In the first place we know that the physical body does not commit sin. It may be the instrument that does the thing, but there is no sin in the physical body itself. If you choose to sin, then you can make your body do it. Sin lies in the will.

Now there isn't any sin in your physical body. There is nothing wrong with your body. It is you, the hidden man of the heart, that makes the body do things that are unseemly and are wrong. Then what does it mean by "sin in the flesh?" For a long time that bothered me. I think I have found a key to it in Verse 11 of this chapter because it is all in one argument. "But if the Spirit of him that raised up Jesus from the dead dwell in you, he that raised up Christ from the dead shall also quicken your mortal bodies by his Spirit that dwelleth in you."

The apostle is not talking about the resurrection He is talking about giving life, healing life, to our physical bodies. Our physical bodies don't need life unless they are sick, do they? That is the conclusion of the argument of Romans 8:1-11 — that is a progressive, single argument. What is he talking about? He is talking about disease, sickness, and the sin that is in the flesh—the sin of a broken law in your body.

Sin is breaking the law—some kind of law; and sin in the body is breaking the law of the body. Disease then is a disease, isn't it? Make it two words—*dis-ease*, broken law, wrecked ease, ease that had been destroyed. Ease is health. *Dis-ease* is sickness. Then God has condemned sin in the flesh, hasn't He? There is no escaping it then; that is just what it means.

Now there are three kinds of sickness: the sickness of the body; the sicknesses of the soul, and the sicknesses of the spirit. The basic sickness is spirit sickness. I venture this, that if you could be healed completely in your spirit every last one of you would be well in your bodies. But the whole problem is cleaning up a man in his spirit.

Your body is tired the moment the spirit is discouraged. Your body breaks down under it. As long as your spirit is triumphant, you are a victor and you can go right on. A man is defeated only when he is defeated in his spirit. When he loses courage, he is whipped. The only way to put the man on his feet again is to renew a right spirit within him. It is to renew the spirit that has been defeated and conquered.

Healing then is on three planes: spiritual healing, soul healing, and body healing. Basically the person that is sick in the body has been sick in the spirit quite a while. It has gotten down into his soul and passed through that into the body.

I cannot tell you brethren what this truth that I am telling you has meant to my life. I now can trace every physical change in my body to a spiritual condition. My body responds to my spirit.

HEALING OF THE SPIRIT FIRST

Let me illustrate. Yesterday I was called to see an eighty-year-old man who had been sick for two years. He had blood poisoning in his teeth, and it had gone through his whole body. I went into his presence with a well spirit, a conquering spirit. When I went back today I saw the effect. His spirit had caught the contagion from me. I had sat by his side and opened the Scriptures, and something in me, from my spirit, flowed into his spirit providing healing. This is perfectly scriptural—out of your inner being, that is your spirit, shall flow rivers of living water. He was a Scotsman very reticent, and didn't respond much; but I knew that it had gone into him. I prayed for him and left. I saw him today, and things had happened in his body. His whole outward demeanor had changed. He had received health from the Lord.

A little while ago a woman sent for me to come to pray for her,

37

and I did not speak to her for a moment. I saw it was not a prayer that she needed for her physical body. I saw that I could not touch her physical body. The thing that she needed was that her spirit be adjusted to the Lord.

Corroding cares come and get in around your spirit life, and it breaks your connection with the Lord. Did you ever see a battery in an auto corroded with something, and the corrosion had eaten off the wires and the starter didn't move? What is the matter? Something is corroded there. You should have kept that battery clean. So is your connection with the Lord. The first real healing is the healing of your spirit—getting your spirit adjusted to the Lord. The spirit is the part that contacts with the Lord. If your spirit is out of harmony and out of condition, you can't get faith for healing.

I saw a young man a little while ago. He was in a desperate condition and required a first-class miracle to touch his life at all. I sat by his side and said, "If you will accept Jesus Christ as your Saviour and confess him as Lord and receive eternal life, you are healed."

He asked, "What do you mean?"

I replied, "Just the moment you are born again, you are healed." For years I have never been afraid to promise that. The moment they are born again, eternal life comes into their spirit. That spirit then can come into the closest relation to the Father, the Great Healer, and the life of God pours down into his spirit, soul, and into his body, and he is immediately touched and made whole.

FAITH A PRODUCT OF YOUR SPIRIT, NOT YOUR INTELLECT

Somebody else's faith may—but as far as you personally are concerned—until your spirit is right, you cannot get healing for your body. May I call your attention to another thing? Faith is a product of your spirit, not of your intellect. Your intellect does not produce faith. Your knowledge may give you ground for faith, but faith is resident in your spirit.

Joy is something in your spirit. Happiness is something that is connected with your surroundings. You are happy because of your surroundings. You are joyful because you are in right relation with the Father. Now faith, love, joy, hope, all spring from your spirit — being the hidden man of the heart. All are products of your spiritual life. The reason that people do not have a rich, beautiful faith is that their spirit is denied the privilege of communion and fellowship with the Father.

Do you understand me? You don't read your Bible; you don't pore over it; you don't live in it; you don't spend any time in fellowship with the Father. Consequently your spirit is depleted and weakened. The faith that grows out of it is a sickly plant. On the other hand, your spirit life is made fruitful and built up and enriched by communion with the Father and by reading His Word. And as your spirit becomes strong and vigorous, there issues from it a faith that is triumphant and creative. I venture to say this, that the men and women who are weak in faith, who once were mighty in faith, are so because they have stopped feeding on the Word of God and stopped intimate, close fellowship with the Father.

Let me say to you with all frankness that you cannot lose your faith until you have broken your fellowship. Just as long as your fellowship is rich and your spiritual life is at flood tide, faith is triumphant. I have followed that in my own life. For years I did not understand the law that governs it. I see it now. You see, here is the thing that is mightily important: that the spirit life in a man is kept healthy and vigorous—kept healthy and vigorous by three exercises. There are more ways, but three in particular:

One is feeding on the Word. Second is a continual public confession of what you are and what Jesus is to you. I am not talking of sin. I mean confession of your faith in Christ, of what Christ is to you, of His fullness, of His completeness, and of His redemption. And the third thing is communion with Him. Feeding on the Word, confession, and communion. Three simple things, aren't they? And yet they are the things that produce great spiritual life. You do not have it without them.

There are three planes of healing: spiritual, mental, and physical. Now for just a bit I want to call to your attention another very important fact: the relation of your body to your spiritual life. Paul said in I Corinthians 9 that he kept his body under, lest haply after he preached to others, he himself would be laid aside—not lost, but laid aside, no longer usable. Why? Because his body had gained the ascendancy over his spiritual life. If you have become a glutton and just live to gratify your appetite by eating and drinking, you will lose out spiritually. But if you will keep your appetite under control, and your body under as Paul said he did, your will will have a chance to evidence itself.

IMPORTANCE OF DAILY READING THE WORD

Now let me state it again: You may be a great spiritual athlete; you may have been a great spiritual athlete, but somewhere you have stopped feeding on the Word. The Word lost its flavor and taste to you. I know of preacher after preacher who had great power at one time, but they have lost all the joy in the Scripture. How do I know? Well, I know by the way they act. When a man loves a woman, he wants her to be with him, doesn't he? He doesn't care to go off and spend evenings alone. And when a man loves his Bible you will find the Bible with him, in his arms, somewhere. He has gotten hold of the thing. He is holding it.

When I find a man along in years, his hair is growing gray, and I see that he loves the Bible, I know that man is fresh in his spirit life.

You can trace the downfall of every spiritual giant that I have ever known in my life to one of these three things: he's lost his desire for the Book. I heard one of the greatest men this country ever produced, when that Book was in his hand, when he preached just like this. He drove me to my knees. Every time I would hear him I would go out, get alone, and pray if I could possibly do it. He filled me, thrilled me, and lifted me. I saw him 20 years later when his name was on the lips of every man. I heard him preach, and I noticed that he quoted a good many Scriptures, but he never picked up his Bible. I noticed he had a theory and a philosophy of redemption instead of the old-time simple exposition of the Word. And I saw that man whose name was known in every part of the world with something like 60 churches sponsoring him in a building that seated about 3500, and the building was not half full. He had the greatest Gospel soloist that this country had ever produced, but the meeting was as dry and dead as any formal service imaginable. I said to the singer who left that field and came with me for a campaign or two, "Charlie, what is the matter with him?"

"Well," he replied, "I don't know, but he is no more like the man he used to be than anything in this world." There had been no sin come into that man's life—his life was just as clean as it had ever been. But here is how it had come: somehow or other he had broken in his spiritual life with the food of the Spirit—the Bible. And the second thing, he used to have the most marvelous prayer life—he didn't have it any more. And the third thing in that whole sermon I didn't hear one personal confession, because he was preaching in a place where personal confession was taboo. People criticized it. If you said anything about yourself and your own experience, the ministers right off the first thing would say, "He is bragging about his own life, isn't he?"

Brother, you will brag about your own life if you have power with God, and you can't help this bragging; you have something to brag about. You have a walk in the fullness of the life and fellowship of your spirit with His spirit, and you have something to talk about, haven't you? Fresh new experiences are coming into you all the time. You are walking in the realm of miracles. I knew that man when he walked in the creative realm of faith. I knew him later when he moved down into the purely intellectual realm.

Healing is basically a spiritual thing. The power that heals the sick comes from God down through your spirit, out through your hands into that man or woman. If you are having the right kind of spiritual fellowship, you will have power with God, and there is no escaping it. But listen, brother, you can't get a powerful current of divine life from a little impoverished wire, can you? And you can't get it when the wire where it connects with you is corroded with worldly cares.

You say, "I will tell you what I want. I want to be able to stand about 10,000 volts. I want to be wired up to God so that the fullness of His power can pour down through me, through my soul, out through my hands and voice to the people."

It doesn't take much to break the connection of your spirit and His. God is a spirit. You are a spirit. Something breaks the connection, and the power no longer flows through. You ask me to pray for you. There is no power. What is the matter? Something has broken the connection. The power comes through the one who prays, but it can't get through your spirit and touch you. But suppose you and I are both right in our spirits. You will get your healing as sure as God sits on His throne. "But if the Spirit of him that raised up Jesus from the dead dwell in you, he that raised up Christ from the dead" shall send healing through your spirit and into your mortal flesh.

The second thing that must be done continually is that after you have fed on the Word, you must open your spirit to confession. You can't bottle up God. He will use you to communicate to others. You act as a medium to communicate Himself to others by message or testimony or prayer. You are His instrument through which He is going to work. Beautiful, isn't it?

Now you see that keeps you in perfect communion because you

41

have to get new messages continually from Him, so you live in perfect fellowship with Him, feeding on His Word and telling of the things He does for you. And no Christian preacher can long survive that does not have a present tense up-to-date testimony. No Christian is safe that hasn't a *now* experience with the Lord because sickness can come on you and you have no power to throw it off.

The relation of your body to your spiritual life is almost an unexplored tableland of possibilities. In Romans 6:12 Paul says, "Let not sin therefore reign in your mortal body." Let not sin reign. But the sin is first in your spirit and in your soul. It is somewhere active in your thinking processes. Then it results in a broken physical law in your body—that is sickness.

A woman said to me recently, "My daughter is determined to have an operation." I asked, "What is the matter with her?" She answered, "The doctor doesn't know, but he thinks he ought to explore in there." Did you ever hear it? And so he is going to cut her open and explore. You turn your body over to be used by the doctors to make money out of, and the surgeons to chop you up for a splendid fee. Great, isn't it! She will go after she is all wrecked, ruined and can't get any healing, and then she will turn to the Lord. Then she will expect to get her healing without asking the Lord's forgiveness for turning her body over to some man for experimentation. "Know ye not that your body is the temple of the Holy Ghost?"

That body of yours is God's holy house, God's holy dwelling place. Why it is the most sacred thing on earth. Now the temple that God designed and gave to Israel in the wilderness contained the Holy of Holies, the inner place. And in that temple that Solomon was permitted to build for God was the Holy of Holies, for the Shekinah Presence dwelt there. The Shekinah Presence now dwells in your body.

THE PARABLE OF THE BEAUTIFUL CHURCH

Can you imagine brethren—here is a beautiful church which cost half a million dollars. It is just a dream of architectural beauty. Everything is in perfect harmony. Wonderful carpets, wonderful furniture, wonderful decorations and the most up-to-date lighting system—everything is perfectly beautiful and artistic. It is a dream of beauty. And they dedicate it to the Lord, and they all go home. They dedicate it on a Saturday. Sunday they are going down to hold their first services in it, and when they open the door they make the most awful discovery—a horrible stench rushes out to meet them. What has happened? I will tell you. A sacrilegious man opened the door last night and drove in a herd of hogs, and the hogs have been staying in that beautiful edifice during the night. It is a horrible thing.

That is just what we do with these bodies of ours. We have dedicated them to God; then we let a flock of unclean thoughts come in, and we let diseases come in and settle in these bodies of ours until these precious bodies that belong to God are filled with the children of these unclean things. Tuberculosis is the child of a thought; it is the product of a mental and spiritual condition. This is true, that when we are in right communion and fellowship with the Lord, there is not power enough in all hell to put disease upon our little finger.

Now beloved, let us go into the thing a little bit farther. The real healing of your life begins in your spirit, doesn't it? Hebrews 7:25 says, "Wherefore he is able also to save them to the uttermost that come unto God by him, seeing he ever liveth to make intercession for them."

Brethren, if God is able to save and to heal to the uttermost, then there are no healings that are impossible, are there? Absolutely none. It dosen't make any difference how sick you are, there is healing for you if you are in contact with the Healer.

"Know ye not that your body is the temple of the Holy Ghost?" Now when that comes to pass, then there come two spirits. There are two spirits in your body now. There was one before; it was a renewed spirit. Then the great mighty Holy Spirit came in. Now you have two spirits in your body, and one soul.

The Holy Spirit wants to dominate your spirit. He wants through your spirit to communicate the unveilings of the Father through the Word to your intellect, and bring your intellect, and your affections into perfect harmony with His will, so that you will yield yourself to Him. You pore over the Book and take it as your own. You read it, feed upon it, you eat it, for it is more necessary than your daily food. "Man shall not live by bread alone, but by every word" and you pore over the Word, meditate upon it, and get at the heart of the thing. Your spiritual nature grows and develops until it dominates your intellect. But if you read just intellectual things, novels, and cheap stories, then your sickly intellect will absolutely

43

dominate your spirit life, break your communion with the Lord, and leave your spirit life in darkness.

What is the way to health? I venture this: it is possible to rebuild your spirit life as you can rebuild a broken body. I have told you how many of the great athletes grow strong. One of them I met years ago was given up to die with tuberculosis. Another of the great athletes, one of the great wrestlers, was given up to die at 18 with tuberculosis. He became one of the outstanding wrestlers in America. What a man can do in his physical body can be done in his spirit, can be done with his intellect. There is absolutely no reason why our spiritual life should not be given up to 100% efficiency.

I wish I were keen enough in my spiritual nature. I'd have a blackboard put behind us, and I'd have someone come that understood art work. I would look over the audience and I'd take each one and I'd say to the artist, "Draw that man's spirit and let me show him his spiritual condition," and you would see your spirit up there. If it were a weak, sickly, puny thing, you would see it. You should see some people when they come in the meeting— their spirits on a stretcher, emaciated, tubercular, no flesh on them — just skinny, horrible looking, living corpses and great, husky bodies. But their spirits are shrinking, feeble, emaciated things. And they come up to me and ask, "Mister, what is the matter with me? I don't seem to have any joy in the Lord." Imagine! I say, "Brother, you have spiritual tuberculosis. Your spirit is emaciated. I don't know whether it will survive the night."

Another comes up to me and asks, "Preacher, what is the matter with me?" I look at him carefully for a moment. "Do you want me to diagnose it?" "Yes sir." "You have a cancer. It is on your spirit; it is laying siege to the jugular vein of your spirit, and I don't think it will be but a little while before it will finish your life. It will kill you right out."

Now if your spirit has reached the place where it has no appetite for the things of God, you have been playing hooky. You have been feeding on things that you ought not to eat, and you have compelled your poor spirit to feed on trash, cheap scandal, useless talk, and wisecracking. You have never given your spirit any real, healthy food for a long time. The poor thing is dying of hunger.

The doctor then told of an experience he had down in Texas where a whole congregation had come, practically all of them for healing. He told them, "You just sit there and listen to me preach, and I won't pray for you at all." He said the largest percentage of that congregation was perfectly healed in just a little while. They came every day for 30 days. At the end of 30 days there was only about 7% of the whole congregation that was not healed. All they did was get healed spiritually. When you get healed spiritually, the chances are a hundred to one you will be healed physically. Do you know I have discovered this: there are quite a number of folk that come to be prayed for, and they are healed over and over again. The healing they need is not physical but spiritual. You get right and get adjusted so that you are feeding on the Word, so that you are enjoying the Bible, so that you are giving a public testimony, and you will be well—or you will be in a condition to get well.

CHAPTER VI

Have Christians a Right to Pray, "If it be thy will" Concerning Sickness?

I purpose this afternoon to speak on this subject, "Have Christians a right to pray, 'If it be thy will' concerning sickness?" I first want to read the Lord's prayer in Luke 11:1-4:

> "And it came to pass, that, as he was praying in a certain place, when he ceased, one of his disciples said unto him, Lord, teach us to pray, as John also taught his disciples. And he said unto them, When ye pray, say, Our Father which art in heaven, Hallowed be thy name. Thy kingdom come. Thy will be done, as in heaven, so in earth. Give us day by day our daily bread. And forgive us our sins; for we also forgive every one that is indebted to us. And lead us not into temptation, but deliver us from evil."

Beloved, if there is one thing in the world I wish I could do for all the people of God, it would be to teach them to pray. Not to teach them to say prayers, but teach them to pray. There is such a mightly lot of difference between saying prayers and praying. "The prayer of faith shall save the sick, and the Lord shall raise him up; and if he has committed sins, they shall be forgiven him."

The prayer of faith has power in it. The prayer of faith has trust in it. The prayer of faith has healing in it for soul and body. The disciples wanted to know how to pray real prayers, and Jesus said unto them, "When ye pray, say, Our Father which art in heaven . . . Thy will be done."

People stop there, and they resign at that point their intelligence to the unknown will of an unknown God. But they have missed the spirit of the prayer. I want to show it to you as it is written in the Word. It does not say, "If it be thy will," and stop there. There is a comma there, not a period. The prayer is, "Thy will be done, as in heaven, so in earth." That is mighty different, isn't it? Not, "Thy will be done." Let the calamity come? Let your children be stricken with fever? Or your son go to the insane asylum? Or your daughter to the home of the feeble-minded? That is not what Jesus was teaching the people to pray. Jesus was teaching the people to pray, "Thy will be done as in heaven, so in earth." Let the might of God be made known. Let the power of God descend. Let God avert the calamity that is coming. Let it be turned aside through faith in God.

How is the will of God done in heaven? For a little while I want your thoughts to be turned with mine heavenward. We step over there, and we look all about the city. We note its beauty and recognize its grandeur. We see the Lamb of God. We do not see a single drunken man on the golden streets, not a single man on a crutch. Not a woman tainted with sin.

HEALING OF THE SOUL, THEN HEALING OF THE BODY

A man came the other day and was telling me what an ardent Christian he was. But after he left, I said, "Lift the windows and let the balance of the man out." Men ought to smell like they pray. We defile ourselves with many things. Recently, a dear man in great distress came to me. He said his eyes were going blind. The physician had told him he had only a year of sight, perhaps less. As I endeavored to comfort him and turn his face toward God, I reverently put my hands on his eyes and asked God for Christ's sake to heal him, and as I did so the Spirit of God kept speaking to my soul and saying, "Amaurosis." I asked, "What is 'amaurosis'?" And as soon as I could get where I could use a dictionary, I looked up the word to see what it meant. It is a disease of the eyes caused by the use of nicotine. That was what was the matter with the man, and the Spirit of the Lord was trying to tell me, but I was too dull and I did not understand. I do not know what the man's name is, but the other day the Lord sent him back to my office, and as we sat together I related the incident to him and said, "My brother, when you quit poisoning yourself, the probabilities are that you may not need any healing from God."

We defile ourselves in various ways. We go on defiling ourselves, and some people are able to stand the defilement a long time and throw it off. Others are not able to; it poisons their system, destroys their faculties. One man may drink whiskey and live to be an old man. Another may go to wrack in a few months or years. Some systems will throw off much; others will not.

Now when we get to the beautiful city, we do not find any of these conditions, so we say, "Angel, tell me what is the reason you do not have any sick up here?" The angel replies, "The will of God is being done here." No sin exists where the will of God is being done. There is no sickness where the will of God is being done.

Then I return to earth, and I can pray the prayer with a new understanding, "Thy will be done in me on earth, as thy will is done in heaven." Just as the will of God is done there, so let the will of God be done here. Let the will of God be done in me. "Thy will be done, as in heaven, so in earth."

But someone says, "Brother do you not remember in Matthew 8, how a leper came to Jesus one day and said to Him, 'Lord, if thou wilt, thou canst make me clean'? The leper said when he prayed, 'If it be thy will,' why should I not say that too?" Well, he was ignorant of what the will of Christ was concerning sickness. Perhaps he had been up on the mountainside and heard Jesus preach that wonderful Sermon on the Mount, for it was at its close that he came to Jesus and said, "If thou wilt, thou canst make me clean."

He knew Christ's ability to heal, but he did not understand His willingness. Jesus' reply settled the question for the leper and should settle the question for every other man forever. Jesus said, "I will; be thou clean." If He had ever said anything else to any other man, there might be some reason for us to interject, "If it be thy will," in our prayers. "If" always doubts. The prayer of faith has no "ifs" in it.

Suppose a drunken man kneels down at this platform and says, "I want to find God. I want to be a Christian." Every man and woman in this house who knows God would say, "Yes," right away. "Tell him to pray, to have faith in God, and God will deliver him." Why do you do it? Simply because there is no question in your mind concerning God's will in saving a sinner who is ready to confess his sin. But you take another step over, and here is a poor fellow by his side with a lame leg; and he comes limping along, kneels down, or tries to, and right away a lot of folks say, "I wish he would send for a doctor," or else they pray, "If it be thy will, make him well," forgetting, "Who forgiveth all thine iniquities; who healeth all thy diseases."

Instead of Christians taking the responsibility, they try to put the responsibility on God. Everything there is in the redemption of Jesus Christ is available for man, when man will present his claim in faith and take it. There is no question in the mind of God

48

concerning the salvation of a sinner. No more is there concerning the healing of a sick one. It is in the atonement of Jesus Christ. His atonement was unto the uttermost, to the last need of man. The responsibility rests purely, solely, and entirely on man. Jesus put it there. Jesus said, "When ye pray, believe that ye receive them, and ye shall have them." And you shall have. No question about it in the words of Jesus.

If ever a man made his words emphatic, it was Jesus. If ever He spoke with emphasis on any question, it was on the subject of God's will, and the result of faith in prayer. Indeed He did not even speak them in ordinary words, but in the custom of the East. He said, "Verily, verily." Amen. The same as if I would stand in an American court and say, "I swear to tell the truth, the whole truth, and nothing but the truth, so help me God." So the Easterner raised his hand and said, "Amen, amen," or "Verily, verily"—with the solemnity of an oath, I say unto you. So Jesus said, "When ye pray, believe that ye receive them, and ye shall have them."

James in expounding the subject says concerning those that doubt, "Let not that man think that he shall receive any thing of the Lord." Why? Well, he says a man that doubteth "is like a wave of the sea driven with the wind and tossed." There is no continuity in his prayer. There is no continuity in his faith. There is no continuity in his character. There is no concentration in God for the thing that he wants. He is like the waves of the sea, scattered and shattered, driven here and there by the wind because there is "if" in it. "Let not that man think that he shall receive anything of the Lord."

That leper did not know what the mind of Jesus was concerning sickness. Perhaps he had seen others healed of ordinary diseases, but leprosy was a terrible thing. It was incurable and contagious. The poor man was compelled as he went down the road to cry out, "Unclean! Unclean!" in order that the people might run away from him.

THE HEALING OF THE LEPERS

In my work in South Africa, I have seen dozens of lepers, hundreds of them, thousands of them. I have seen them with their fingers off at the first joint, at the second joint, with their thumbs off, or noses off, their teeth gone, the toes off, the body scaling off, and I have seen God heal them in every stage. On one occasion in our work, a company of healed lepers gathered on Christmas eve and partook of the Lord's Supper. Some had no fingers on their hands, and they had to take the cup between their wrists, but the Lord had been there and had healed them. That was not under my ministry, but under the ministry of a poor, black fellow, who five or six years before did not even wear pants. He wore a great goat skin apron. But he came to Christ. He touched the living One. He received the power of God and manifested a greater measure of the real healing gift than I believe any man ever had in modern times. And if I were with him now, I would kneel down and ask that black man to put his hands on my head and ask God to let the same power of God come into my life that He has in his.

You have no more right to pray, "If it be thy will" when you kneel to pray concerning your sickness than the leper had. Not as much, because for two thousand years the Word of God has been declared, and the Bible has been an open book. We ought to be intelligent beyond any other people in the world concerning the mind of God.

"But brother," someone says, "you have surely forgotten that when Jesus was in the garden He prayed, 'Father, if it be possible, let this cup pass from me: nevertheless not as I will, but as thou wilt'." No, I have not forgotten. You are not the Saviour of the world, beloved. That was Jesus' prayer. No other man ever could pray that prayer but the Lord Jesus. But I want to show you, beloved, what caused Jesus to pray that prayer, because a lot of folk have never understood.

Jesus had gone into the garden to pray. The burden of His life was upon Him. He was about to depart. He had a message for the world. He had been compelled to commit it to a few men — ignorant fishermen. I believe that He wondered, "Will they be able to present the vision? Will they see it as I have seen it? Will they be able to let the people have it as I have given it to them?" No doubt these were some of His inquiries, and many more.

Do you know what the spirit of intercession is? Do you know what it means when a common man comes along, as Moses did, and takes upon himself the burden of the sin of the people and then goes down in tears and repentance unto God, until the people are brought back in humility and repentance to his feet? When in anxiety for his race and people, Moses said, in essence, "Lord if you forgive not this people, blot my name out of thy book."

Think of it! Moses took upon himself that responsibility and said to God, "If you forgive not this people, blot my name out of thy book." God heard Moses' prayer, bless God!

Paul on one occasion wrote practically the same words: "I could wish that myself were accursed from Christ for my brethren, my kinsmen according to the flesh." He felt the burden of his people. So Jesus in the Garden felt the burden of the world, the accumulated sorrows of mankind, their burdens of sin, their burdens of sickness. And as He knelt to pray, His heart breaking under it, the great drops of sweat came out on His brow like blood, falling down to the ground. But the critics have said, "It was not blood." But I tell you I knew a man who sweated blood.

THE EXPERIENCE OF JUDGE V. V. BARNES

Judge V. V. Barnes in his great trial before Judge Landis actually sweat blood until his handkerchief would be red with the blood that oozed through his pores. His wife said that for three months she was compelled to put napkins over his pillow. That is one of the biggest men God has ever let live in the world. His soul was big, and he saw the possibility of the hour for a great people and desired as far as he could to make that burden easy for them. He did not want the estate to go into the hands of a receiver. The interests of one hundred thousand people were in his hands. The accumulated properties of families who had no other resource were at stake. He was so large that the burden of the heart bore down on him so that he sweat blood and did so for three months.

But the people in these days say, "It looked like blood," and are so teaching their Sunday school scholars. The Lord have mercy on them! The blood came out, and it fell down on the ground.

Jesus thought He was going to die right there in the Garden, but He was too big to die there. He wanted to go on to the cross. He wanted to see this thing finished on behalf of the race of man, and so He prayed, "Father, if it be possible, let this cup pass from me: nevertheless, not as I will, but as thou wilt." What was the cup? Was it the cup of suffering that was breaking Him down, that was draining out the lifeblood right then, and that would be His death instead of the cross? But He towered above that and prayed, "Father, if it be possible, let this cup pass from me: nevertheless. not as I will, but as thou wilt." Instantly God heard His prayer. Instantly the angels came and ministered to Him, and in the new strength He received, He went on to the cross and to His death as the Saviour of mankind.

Beloved, I want to tell you, if there were a little more sweating of blood and of that kind of praying, there would be less sickness and sin than there is. God is calling for a people who will take upon them that kind of a burden and let the power of God work through them.

THE HEALING OF A WOMAN WITH A BROKEN BACK

People look in amazement in these days when God answers prayer for a soul. A week ago last night my dear wife and I went to pray for a soul, a Mrs. McFarland. Ten years ago a tree fell on her and broke her back. She became paralyzed, and for ten years she has been in a wheel chair, her limbs swollen, and her feet a great senseless looking lump that hang down useless. She says that many preachers have visited her in these years and have told her to be reconciled to the will of God, sit still, and suffer longer. She said, "Oh I would not mind waiting. If the pain would just stop for a little while, it would be so good. I would feel as if I were rewarded."

We lovingly laid our hands upon her and prayed. You ask, "Did you pray, 'If it be thy will'?" No! I did not, but I laid my hands on that dear soul and prayed, "You devil that has been tormenting this woman for ten years and causing the tears to flow, I rebuke you in the name of the Son of God. And by the authority of the Son of God I cast you out."

Something happened. Life began to flow into her being, and the pain left. In a little while she discovered that power coming back into her body. Then she found she could get up on her hands and knees. She began to call in her neighbors and relatives to show them what God had done and how God had delivered her.

AN ALLEGORY OF BEELZEBUB AT THE
DEATH OF CHRIST

May I relate to you something I read in the New Testament Apocrypha? These writings were presented at the Council of Nice, but they were not accepted. Yet there are some interesting things in them. It may be only an allegory, but in the Book of Nicodemus there is a setting of one of the stories that reads like this:

After the crucifixion of Jesus Christ, you remember as one of the recorded miracles which took place at His crucifixion, that many of the saints that were dead arose and appeared in the city.

52

Not a few, but many. There were some who were known to the high priest, and so the high priest took two of these men into the temple and examined them concerning their presence and wanted them to describe what took place in the region of death when Christ was crucified. So they proceeded to describe as best as they could. In the regions of death it was already known that Christ was likely to be crucified and brought to this region. There was great rejoicing among the saints. Isaiah said, "Did I not say so?" "Did I not prophesy so?" asked Zechariah. They were all being reminded of these things, and the rejoicing among them was going on. Presently Beelzebub, who is the keeper of the regions of death and all the regions of darkness, came on the scene. Shortly Satan appeared and announced to Beelzebub to prepare—that Jesus was about to be crucified. A conversation arose between Beelzebub, the keeper, and Satan. Beelzebub said to him, "Satan, is not this the Jesus of Nazareth, who in His divine nature was so strong that He came here and forcibly took Lazarus when he was here, and we could not hold him?"

Satan answered, "Yes, that is the same man." Then Beelzebub said, "If His divine nature is so strong that He forcibly took Lazarus and we could not hold him, how shall we hold Him?"

That seemed to be a new suggestion to the mind of the evil one. He had never before thought of such a thing as that. And the question, "What shall we do with Him?" was asked.

Beelzebub said, "Keep Him out."

But the Christ appeared and broke down the gates and came in —not as a captive—but as a victor. He took the old saints with Him to His own glory. He is the triumphant Christ. So Beelzebub ended this controversy with these words, "Satan, behold! All things which thou has gained through the forbidden tree, thou has lost through the work of the cross."

The redemption of Christ was an uttermost redemption, to the last need of the human heart—for body, soul, and spirit. He is a Christ and Saviour, even unto the uttermost. Blessed be His Name! Who shall dare to raise a limit to the power of God! Who shall dare to raise a limit to the accomplishment of faith through Jesus Christ? I am glad that the days are passing quickly when men no longer desire to raise barriers before the souls of men. The tendency is to take down the barriers and let all the faith of your heart go out to God, for every man and every condition of life—to let the love of God flow out of your soul to every hungry soul.

You listen to me. Instead of praying, "Lord, if it be thy will," when you kneel beside your sick friend, Jesus Christ has commanded you and every believer to lay your hands on the sick. This is not my ministry alone, nor my brethren's. It is the ministry to every believer. And if your ministers do not believe it, God have mercy on them, and if your churches do not believe it, God have mercy on them.

In these days the churches are screaming and crying because Christian Science is swallowing up the world and that it is false, etc. Why do the people go to Christian Science? They go because they cannot get any truth where they are. Let the day come when the voices of men ring out and tell the people the truth about the Son of God, who is a Redeemer, even unto the uttermost—for body, soul, and spirit. He redeems back to God. Beloved, believe it and receive the blessing that will come into your own life.

CHAPTER VII

The Power of a Christian

A true Christian is unique. He stands alone. He supersedes all who have gone before. He will not have a successor. He is man at his best, and God's best effort for mankind.

When the conception of a Christian has been established within our spirits as the New Testament establishes the ideal Christian, we will understand then how it is that men have been ready to abandon all else in the world in order to attain Christ, to attain His character, and to partake of His Spirit.

I went to South Africa in a most unique time in that nation's history—just after the reconstruction period following the Boer War. Because of the great war, the native populace had been practically frightened out of the country. They had gone far back from the war zone, and the war zone covered practically the whole country.

The gold mines were depending on the natives for labor, and it had become a great issue. How was it possible to carry on the work while this condition of fear rested upon the natives? Finally it was proposed that they should bring in 100,000 men from China. They were brought on a contract for three years. They were a real living colony. They brought their teachers, preachers, priests and prophets.

At the same period the East Indians, who live in South Africa, felt they were not receiving the attention from the government in the way of education that they ought to, so the British Government sent teachers, both religious and secular, to supply them.

The Buddhists, the Yogi, and Confucianists and many others made their headquarters at Johannesburg. Our ministry was unique. We were the only ones who held divine healing services and preached on the subject of healing.

After a little while it dawned on me that here was a possibility that had never come into my life before. If I could get these priests and teachers of the various religions to come together, we might have an exchange of thought. It would at least give me an

55

opportunity to discuss the subject. I was familiar to some extent with Eastern religions, but I had never had any touch with their soul life.

So after some time the matter was arranged. At the same time we added to our company a rabbi from Chicago, Dr. Hearst. We had a combination, I presume, representing all the great religions on earth. We were able by wise exchange and guidance and much prayer to bring about a condition of fellowship, that they spoke out of their hearts to each other with a great deal of freedom.

It had this effect upon me, that these men were groping after light. One thing surely was demonstrated, that in Jesus Christ there is divine life, of which when a man becomes possessor he has a richer and greater appreciation of His power than any other man possesses.

I am convinced that there is a profound secret in the life and character, teaching and virtue of Jesus Christ that when a man attains it, he is rich indeed beyond measure.

Among my young friends in South Africa were two young men whom I have regarded as among the brightest youths I have ever known. One was a Boer. His name was Von Shield. He was the son of an old line stock of highly-educated Hollanders. The other's name was Kratzmall. He had come from a generation of Church of England preachers. He has always stood out in my mind as a sort of counterpart of St. Paul. I think he was more largely duplicated in that man than in any other I ever knew.

Von Shield was a book agent in South Africa. He began to attend our meetings, and one day when I was not present he came forward out of the audience and knelt at the altar and sought God for a conscious knowledge of salvation. And bless God, he received it.

Some days after that when I was present and teaching at an afternoon service, he raised up in his seat and said, "Lake, do you suppose that if God gave me the baptism of the Holy Spirit it would satisfy the burning yearning that is in my soul for God?" I said, "My son, I don't know that it would, but I think it would go a long piece on the way."

So without more ado he came forward, knelt and looking up said to me, "Lay your hands on my head and pray." And as I did the Spirit of God descended in an unusual manner. He was baptized in the Holy Ghost very wonderfully indeed and became a transformed man. From that hour that man was a living personification of the power of God. All my life I have never found one through whom such majestic intense flashes of power would come as through that soul at intervals.

Presently he disappeared. His father came to me, saying, "I am troubled about Harry. He took a Bible and went off into the mountains almost three weeks ago. I am afraid he is going insane." I said, "Brother, do not worry yourself. One of these days he will come down in the power and glory of God." I knew what was in that fellow's heart.

One day he returned under such an anointing of the Spirit as I have never before witnessed on any life. Not long after that he came to me and said, "Brother Lake, did you know this was in the Bible?" And he proceeded to read to me that familiar verse in the 16th chapter of Mark: "These signs shall follow them that believe; In my name shall they cast out devils." Looking up into my face with great earnestness, he said, "My! I wish I knew somebody that had a devil!"

AN AMAZING CASE OF DELIVERANCE

I believe God had planned that situation, for I was reminded that in my mail a couple of days before had come a request for an insane son. The mother said, "As far as I can tell my son has a devil," and her request was that we might come and pray that the devil might be cast out. He said, "Why this is only a couple or three blocks from where I live. I am going to find this fellow and then I am coming back for you."

I said to myself, "Here is a newborn soul, whose vision enters into the real realm of God-power." I realized that my own spirit had not touched the degree of faith that was in that soul, and I said to myself, "I do not want to say a word or do a thing that will discourage that soul in the least."

Presently he came back and said, "Brother Lake, come on." We went and found a boy who had been mad from his birth; he was like a wild animal. He would not wear clothes and would smash himself or anybody else with anything that was given him. He couldn't even have a dish to eat on. But in the center of the enclosure where he was they had a large stone hollowed out and they would put his food in that and let him eat it just like an animal.

We tried to catch him, but he was wild as a lion. He would jump right over my head. Finally his father said, "You will not catch him out there." I had been somewhat of an athlete in my youth and I said to Von Shield, "You get on one side and if he comes to your side you will take care of him, and if he comes to my side I will take care of him."

Now beloved, this all sounds strange I know, but I'll never forget that afternoon as long as I live. As I looked across to that young man I could see the lightning flash of faith, and I knew that if he got his hands on that man that devil would come out.

Presently he landed on my side of the bed, and in an instant Von Shield sprang over the bed, laid his hands on his head and commanded the devil to come out. In two minutes that man was absolutely transformed, and was a sane man, the first moment of sanity he ever knew.

THE STRANGE CHALLENGE OF VON SHIELD

One more incident in the man's life that will help you to realize what God had done for him. The Boer people were a pioneer people. They did not have the advantages of good schools. About the only educated person in a community was the Dutch Predicant. He was a real aristocrat, with all the authority that the priests of Ireland exercised over the people there. One day Von Shield was conducting a service with a couple of hundred people present. The predicant was there. He arose as he was teaching and told the people that they were being misled, and that these things Von Shield was talking about were only calculated for the days of the apostles.

If Von Shield had been an ordinary young man he would have been somewhat nonplussed. But presently he said, "I will tell you how we will settle this thing. There is Miss LeRoux whom we all know. She is stone blind in one eye, and has been for four years. I will ask her to come here and I will lay hands upon her and ask the Lord Jesus to make her well." And picking up his Dutch Bible, he said to her, "And when He heals you, you will read that chapter," designating the chapter she was to read.

God Almighty met the fellow's faith; the woman's eye opened right then, and she stood before that congregation and covering the good eye, read with the eye that had been blind, the entire chapter.

KRATZMALL RECEIVES THE HOLY GHOST

Now I will return to Kratzmall, the other young man. He was visiting one night at the home of some friends, a few doors from my house. These young people with whom he was visiting had just recently been baptized in the Spirit themselves, and they were very anxious about this friend, and had been praying a great deal about it. This same night he was in the tabernacle and his friends said, "Come down to our home." So he went.

After a time it was suggested that they pray. Kratzmall said in speaking of it afterwards, "It was not my custom to kneel. But as I sat in my chair I began to realize that a peculiar power was taking hold of me. I said this must be some sort of psychological condition that I am not familiar with. Anyway, I will have nothing to do with it." The Spirit of God intensified, but he was determined not to yield. For two hours and a half he sat there while the perspiration poured off his person. But at the end of this time the battle was going on, a voice spoke within him and said, "I am Jesus." And instantly he said, "If you are Christ you can do anything you like." The next moment the Spirit of God deepened on him and he began to speak in tongues by the power of God.

Kratzmall, after that anointing, became one of the most remarkable preachers of the Gospel I have ever known anything about. He traveled that country from end to end when he didn't have a cent. I met him once when he had no shoes, and his feet were cut and bleeding. But he established congregations of Christian people for 350 miles down through the wilderness.

I have told you these incidents in order to demonstrate to you that there is a force in the Christian life that mankind has not taken hold of in any great degree. And the thing that interests me most is the inquiry that comes to me day by day from souls with whom I deal in the healing room: "How can I enter into the consciousness of the presence and power of Christ?"

That is the real issue in all our hearts. We see the thing that was burning in the heart of Nicodemus when he came to Jesus in the night time and said, "Master, we know that thou art a teacher come from God, for no man could do the miracles that thou doest, except God be with him." But Jesus, disregarding all that, said, "Except a man be born again he cannot see the kingdom of God. . . . That which is born flesh is flesh; and that which is born of the Spirit is spirit. Marvel not that I said unto thee, Ye must be born again."

The birth-again of God, the conscious incoming of the Spirit of God into the life and being and personality, lifts mankind out of the condition of normal Christian experience into the place of divine consciousness and power.

The baptism of the Holy Spirit was the common experience of New Testament times. The New Testament was written by men who had the baptism of the Holy Ghost. It was written to churches that possessed the baptism of the Holy Ghost. Indeed in my study of the New Testament the disciples seemed to consider it essential that each individual should possess the baptism of the Spirit. When

Paul came down to Ephesus the first question he asked them was, "Have ye received the Holy Ghost since ye believed?" And they said, "We have not as much as heard whether there be any Holy Ghost," but they had been baptized unto John's baptism. Then he explained to them what John's baptism was and that "John verily baptized with the baptism of repentance, saying unto the people that they should believe on Him which should come after him, that is, on Christ Jesus." Then he laid his hands upon them and they received the Holy Ghost, and began to speak with tongues and prophesy. There were similar cases at Samaria and the house of Cornelius.

I tell you it is my conviction at this hour that this is the real manner in which the Lord desires to pour out the Spirit in these days. We have had many services in which the power fell on the people as they sat hearing the Word of God. I have witnessed the Lord baptize 50 people in an ordinary service on Sunday evening.

There is a consciousness of sinlessness that enables a person to enter into the direct presence of God—the consciousness that your sins are gone. You can classify sin in any way you like. There is this much about it, that in our own inner soul we know that sin is offensive to God because it is offensive to our own spirit.

Indeed I remember in my own experience when my heart began to be stirred along this line, and I definitely began to seek for the baptism of the Holy Spirit, that as the illumination of the purity and holiness of God began to dawn over my soul, there was an inclination to draw back as I realized the awful extreme between my own heart and the heart of God. And I was compelled to cry out, yea not once, but a thousand times, "Lord, by the divine process of God cleanse my soul from this condition." And I remember how that one night I was present in Fred Bosworth's home, and an ordinary meeting was going on conducted by a little Quaker woman. She outlined to me what seemed to me to be the method of cleansing of the soul.

That night as I knelt there, the consciousness of the cleansing power of Jesus Christ went through my being, and I realized something of what I never realized before, that the battle between my spirit and my soul had ceased, and that God reigned, not only in my spirit but in my flesh, too. The war that had been in my spirit for years was all gone, and I entered into Beulah land; and I really felt that I had crossed the Jordan and everything was new.

In the 17th verse of the fourteenth chapter of John, Jesus was discussing this subject with the disciples. He said, "He is with you," that is, the Comforter. "He is with you, and shall be in you." There is a place where the individual becomes the conscious recipient of the Spirit of God. Indeed the Word of God puts it in this forceful manner: "Know ye not that your body is the temple of the Holy Ghost which is in you?" It is God's purpose that man shall be the conscious possessor of the Spirit of the living God.

That is the real Christian. That is the thing that has been lacking in the Church throughout the centuries that are past. It was that consciousness of God's presence and God's power in the disciples and the Church of the first centuries that wrote across the pages of history that wonderful, wonderful record of Christianity of the first four hundred years.

Did you ever think of it that in the first four centuries there were thirty million Christian martyrs? Thirty million gave up their lives for Christ! There was a spirit that made it so intense, so powerful, that had such power that the world got out. But there came a day when the Church traded the communion of the Holy Ghost for the smile of the world, and then the long, long night of the middle centuries followed.

We are living in a day and hour when the Spirit of God has come into the world afresh, when the consciousness of mankind is opening up to God in a manner that they have never opened before. There is an awakening in the world from ocean to ocean, from pole to pole, as there never was before. And I believe that God Almighty's outpouring of the Spirit upon all flesh is at hand. And though we are receiving the drippings, and our own hearts are being warmed by the impulse of the Spirit, that day is not far distant when the flame of God will catch the soul of mankind and the Church of the latter day will close this era with a place of divine glory excelling that of the Early Church.

This is according to the prophecy of the Word: "If the former rain was abundant, shall not the latter rain be more abundant?" If the disciples without the train of Christian history behind them that you and I have, were able to enter into the divine consciousness and power of the Holy Spirit in such a way that they left a stamp upon all Christianity, how much more shall men and women who have the advantage of 2,000 years of Christian record, enter into a divine consciousness that even the apostles possessed!

Christ For The Nations
Magazine

FREE*
One Year Subscription

Christ For The Nations monthly magazine includes motivational articles, an informative "World Prayer & Share Letter," a missions project, updates regarding CFN's anointed conferences and news about what's happening at CFN's interdenominational Bible institute, which trains world changers for the 21st century.
Please send request to:

Christ For The Nations ● P.O. Box 769000 ● Dallas, TX 75376-9000
(214) 376-1711 l www.cfni.org

Please include your name, address, phone, e-mail and date of birth.
*Overseas subscriptions, please pay $10.00.